# INTERMEDIATE
# Grammar

## The *Using Your Language* series

*Elementary Grammar: A Child's Resource Book*

*Intermediate Grammar: A Student's Resource Book*

*Grammar Handbook for Home and School*

The *Using Your Language* series is specially designed to provide young people with home resource books. These guides serve as references in the area of English grammar. They offer clear explanations of critical communication skills to students throughout their school careers.

## Other books by Carl B. Smith

*Expand Your Child's Vocabulary*
*Help Your Child Read and Succeed*
*A Commitment to Critical Thinking*
*Teacher as Decision-Maker*

**To order these books or to receive a catalog of Grayson Bernard publications please write to:**

**Grayson Bernard Publishers**
**223 S. Pete Ellis Dr., Suite 12**
**Bloomington, Indiana 47408**

**or call (800) 925-7853**

# INTERMEDIATE
# Grammar

## A Student's Resource Book

## by Carl B. Smith, Ph.D.

GRAYSON BERNARD
PUBLISHERS

Cover Design by Addie Seabarkrob

Library of Congress Cataloging-in-Publication Data
Smith, Carl Bernard.
    Intermediate grammar: a student's resource book / by Carl B.
Smith
        p. cm. -- (Using your language series)
    Includes index.
    Summary: A guide to English grammar, discussing such
elements as sentence structure, parts of speech, irregular verbs.
    ISBN 0–9628556–3–4: $16.95
    1. English language--Grammar--1950- -- Juvenile literature.
[1. English language--Grammar.]    I. Title    II. Series.
PE1112.S55    1993        428.2--dc20            92–3659

Grayson Bernard Publishers
223 S. Pete Ellis Drive, Suite 12
P. O. Box 5247
Bloomington, Indiana  47407

# Contents

# Contents

## Contents

## 5   Adjectives . . . . . . . . . . . . . . . . . . . . . 93

## 6   Adverbs . . . . . . . . . . . . . . . . . . . . . . . 117

# 7 Function Words: Prepositions and Conjunctions ..... 135

# 8 More about Verbs .................... 155

# Contents

# Introduction

Most of us have occasional questions about the use of the English language. We may say (or hear others say) "Who were you talking to?" or "She went with Mary and I." Do these sentences follow the principles of correct (standard) grammar?

When such questions arise, most people have two needs. One is for a quick answer to the immediate question (the sentences should read "To whom were you talking?" and "She went with Mary and me"). The other is for examples and practice activities that help to make standard grammar a natural part of everyday written and spoken language. This book fills both of those needs.

### Why is it important to understand English grammar?

As a rule, we want to write and to speak correctly—that is, in a manner acceptable to educated people. But aside from being "correct," there is an even more important reason for understanding how English works: to **guide us toward greater clarity of written and spoken language.** Correct grammar helps us express our ideas *clearly* and communicate more *effectively* with others.

As we try to improve communication, we need a vocabulary that enables us to talk about sentences, about types of words, and especially about relationships among words in the sentence. By knowing the individual parts of speech—nouns, verbs, adjectives, and so on—and by understanding how subjects and predicates, phrases and clauses work together, we can discuss ways to improve our sentences and to deliver our messages more clearly.

This resource book will help students, teachers, and parents deal with questions of precision and clarity. It explains the principles of English grammar and gives example sentences to show how to apply them. Each section of the book offers a series of exercises that clarify and put into practice the grammatical principles of that section. Parents and children can use these activities to explore further their questions about speech or writing.

### How should I use this book?

*Intermediate Grammar* is not a school textbook. However, it does cover most of the grammar that students encounter in the middle and upper grades. It is a resource book that can be used in several ways.

# *Introduction*

1. **To find quick answers to questions**

    Use *Intermediate Grammar* just as you use a dictionary or encyclopedia or other reference source. When specific questions arise ("What is an *object pronoun?*" or "When do we use *who* and when do we use *whom?*"), you can check the index to find the pages on which each topic is discussed.

2. **To gain a better understanding of sentence structure**

    If you want to find a more extensive discussion of a topic such as the relationship between subject and verb, you can again check the index to find information and examples relating to your question.

3. **To study or review a grammatical principle**

    You can read complete chapters when you want to understand more about a broad topic. This study can be undertaken
    - at home
    - in a home-school curriculum, or
    - in a support role in school.

The first seven chapters cover material that is usually presented in grades five through eight: basic sentence structure and the functions of the parts of speech. Chapters eight and nine deal more extensively with verbs and with more complicated sentence structures; this material usually appears in grades seven and eight and continues through the upper grades. Chapter ten gives more detailed information on word structure, with emphasis on the function and meaning of prefixes and suffixes. This material can be used at any point in the intermediate or upper grades to suit the interests and needs of each student.

Many questions of punctuation are considered throughout the book and are listed in the index. In addition, you will find a separate Punctuation Guide near the end of the book. This allows you to look in one place for brief explanations of the most important elements of punctuation.

In addition to *Intermediate Grammar,* you can turn to another book entitled *Grammar Handbook for Home and School.* There you will find brief answers to the most important questions about English usage. After you have mastered the material in *Intermediate Grammar,* you can use the explanations in the *Grammar Handbook* for a quick review if any questions arise. Use both of these books to help you work toward the most important goal of language study: clear, effective communication.

# 1

# Sentences

You already know that sentences are groups of words that express complete thoughts. Good sentences are clearly organized so that they make sense to the reader.

## ■ 1a    Subject and Predicate

The most important parts of any sentence are the **subject** and the **predicate**.

> • The **subject** of the sentence is the person or thing the sentence is about. The subject often tells *who* or *what* is doing something in the sentence.
> • The **predicate** of the sentence says something about the subject. It tells what the subject *is* or what the subject is *doing*.*

In the next group of sentences you see a short vertical line between the subject and predicate. The *subject* contains all the words that come before the line, and the *predicate* contains all the words that come after the line.

My room | is a mess.

One night a bear and an ape | were arguing.

I | have a horse named Beauty.

One day four friends | were walking down a country lane.

---

* In this book you will often see some words highlighted in slanted letters called *italics* and other words highlighted in darker letters called **boldface**. Remember that *italics* and **boldface** refer to these two types of printing.

**1**

# Types of Sentences

> - All sentences begin with a **capital letter**.
> - All sentences end with a **punctuation mark** which lets the reader know that the sentence has been completed.
> - There are four types of sentences: *declarative, interrogative, imperative,* and *exclamatory.*

## ■ 1b    Declarative Sentences

> - **Declarative sentences** make statements or give information to the reader. The word *declare* means "to announce or make something known."
> - A **period** (.) is used at the end of a declarative sentence.

The subject often comes near the beginning of the declarative sentence. The predicate makes up the rest of the sentence; it contains the verb as well all the other words needed to complete the meaning of the sentence.

We | went up to our room and got ready.

My career choice | is freelance photography.

I | play soccer, baseball, football, and basketball.

My family and I | came to America two years ago.

## ■ 1c    Interrogative Sentences

> - **Interrogative sentences** ask for information.
>   The word *interrogate* means "to ask questions."
> - A **question mark** (?) is used at the end of an interrogative sentence.

Interrogative sentences often begin with a verb or with a word such as *who* or *why* or *when*.

Does anybody know where we are?

Why didn't you tell me they had left?

Are you through with this book?

Who was knocking on the door?

## ■ 1 d    Imperative Sentences

> • **Imperative sentences** tell or ask someone to *do* something. The word *imperative* means "urgent" or "absolutely necessary."
> • A **period** (.) is used at the end of an imperative sentence.

Here are a few examples of imperative sentences:

Read my lips.

Close the windows before it rains.

Don't fall over those bricks.

Watch for that loose board on the steps.

You can see that the subject is not specified in these sentences. This is because the request is usually addressed directly to a particular person. It is not necessary to say "*You* read my lips" or "*Ellen,* close the windows."

Some imperative sentences are used to alert someone or ask them to do something right away, but other imperative sentences may not be quite so urgent. You may ask someone to do something by using the word *please* at the beginning of the sentence.

Please bring my books over here.

Please close the door when you leave.

**1**

■ **1e    Exclamatory Sentences**

> • **Exclamatory sentences** make strong statements. When you *exclaim*, you express fear or excitement or surprise or some other strong feeling.
> • An **exclamation mark** (!) is used at the end of an exclamatory sentence.

I'm glad that's over!

My tooth is killing me!

That was an incredible game!

I had no idea he could do *that!*

# Simple Sentences

All the examples you have seen so far have been **simple sentences**. Even sentences that contain a number of words in the predicate will be *simple sentences* if they fit the following definition:

> • A **simple sentence** contains *one **complete** subject* and *one **complete** predicate*. A simple sentence expresses *one complete thought*.

■ **1f    The Complete Subject and the Complete Predicate**

> • The **complete subject** includes *all* the words in the subject of a sentence.
> • The **complete predicate** includes the verb and *all* the other words in the predicate of a sentence.

In each of the following sentences, the **complete subject** is separated from the **complete predicate** by a short vertical line. In these sentences the *verb* (written in italics) is the first word in each complete predicate.

| Complete Subject | | Complete Predicate |
|---:|:---:|:---|
| I | \| | *hate* Monday. |
| Life | \| | *is* both good and bad. |
| Some people | \| | *have* a lot of problems. |
| The weather here in Texas | \| | *seems* unreal. |
| One day my best friend and I | \| | *went* to an old junkyard. |
| Suddenly a weird animal | \| | *appeared* before me. |
| For the next hour we | \| | *flew* all around the country. |

When you understand these two parts of the sentence, you can be sure that your sentences always make sense.

## ■ 1g   The Simple Subject

Even though a complete subject may contain several words, there is often one word that is particularly significant. This is called the **simple subject**.

> • The **simple subject** is the most important single word in the complete subject. The simple subject tells *exactly* who or what the sentence is about. The simple subject is often a *noun* or a *pronoun*.

In the next group of sentences, the end of the complete subject is marked by a short vertical line. Within the complete subject you will see the simple subject printed in boldface.

A big green **monster** | slithered out of the spaceship.

The next morning, the **sun** | was shining brightly.

**We** | packed a lot of stuff into the trailer.

After the rain stopped, **I** | dashed out to the car.

In each of the first two sentences the simple subject is a noun: *monster* and *sun*. In each of the last two sentences the simple subject is a pronoun: *We* and *I*.

## ■ 1h The Simple Predicate

The complete predicate may also contain a number of words, but there is usually one word or one small group of words that is most important. This is the **simple predicate**.

> • The **simple predicate** contains the most important word or words in the complete predicate. These important words form the **verb** that tells exactly what the subject *is* or what it *does*.

In the following sentences, a short vertical line separates the complete subject from the complete predicate. Within the complete predicate, the simple predicate is printed in *italics*. This simple predicate is the verb that tells what happens. Notice that the verb may contain more than one word.

The aliens | *tried* to stop us.

Next week we | *will go* on a trip.

Mark Twain | *is* my favorite author.

The old man | *greeted* me in an excited voice.

The workers | *have repaired* the hole in the road.

Later we will see how to combine subjects or predicates to write different kinds of sentences.

## ■ 1i    Diagramming Simple Sentences

In order to understand how sentences are constructed, it is often helpful to make a *diagram*. In a diagram, the most important words in the sentence are written on a *base line*. Then the other words in the sentence can be shown as they relate to the words on the base line.

In many simple sentences, the most important words are the *simple subject* and the verb that makes up the *simple predicate*. In a diagram, the subject and verb are separated by a vertical line that goes through the base line. Here are some short sentences followed by diagrams which show the simple subject and the simple predicate:

My dog ate all the pizza.

| dog | ate |
← *base line*

My friends went with me to the game.

| friends | went |

The <u>people</u> next door are leaving for a week.

| people | are leaving |

In later chapters we will use more elaborate diagrams to see how other parts of the sentence relate to the subject and verb.

## ■ 1j    Compound Subjects

Look at this pair of simple sentences. In each sentence the simple subject is printed in boldface.

**Mary** got a big reward.

**Her brother** got a big reward.

These sentences tell us about two people who did the same thing. Because the *predicate* of each sentence is the same, we can combine the subjects and write a single sentence like this:

**Mary and her brother** got a big reward.

Now the simple subject (*Mary*) from the first sentence has been joined to the simple subject (*brother*) from the second sentence. By using the word *and*, we have written a new sentence with a **compound subject**.

> • A **compound subject** contains two or more simple subjects joined by a word such as *and* or *or*. All parts of the compound subject have the same predicate.

In the next two examples you will see how the subjects of two simple sentences can be combined to form a compound subject. You can do this when both sentences have the same predicate that tells about two or more people who are doing the same thing. After each group of sentences you will see an illustration that shows how the compound subject relates to the complete predicate of the sentence.

**Evan** liked the movie. **Joan** liked the movie.
**Evan and Joan** liked the movie.

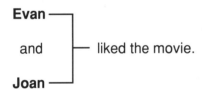

My **friend** learned to swim. **I** learned to swim.
My **friend and I** learned to swim.

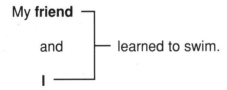

The following example shows how the words in the compound subject can be joined with *or* to show contrast.

**Ellen** will help you finish. **I** will help you finish.
**Ellen or I** will help you finish.

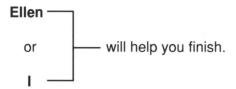

Ellen
or     will help you finish.
I

### ■ 1k    Compound Predicates

When two sentences tell that the same subject is doing two different things, the predicates can be combined using a word such as *and*. Just be sure that the two sentences belong together and make sense when they are joined. All the verbs are printed in *italics* in the next example.

> Sue *stood* at the window. Sue *watched* for the bus.
> Sue *stood* at the window and *watched* for the bus.

The last sentence has a **compound predicate**. The subject (*Sue*) from each of the shorter sentences is used only once because the two verbs (*stood* and *watched*) both tell what she did.

> • A **compound predicate** contains two or more simple predicates joined by a word such as *and*. All parts of the compound predicate have the same subject.

We are still writing **simple sentences** that express one complete thought. Even though the predicate contains two important verbs, these verbs still work together to form one complete predicate. Remember that a **simple sentence** has one *complete* subject and one *complete* predicate.

In the following examples you will see how the predicates of two simple sentences can be combined to form a **compound predicate**. Each set of sentences tells about one subject that did two different things. Again, the illustration after each group of sentences shows how the subject relates to the words in the compound predicate.

> The squirrel *gathered* nuts. The squirrel *buried* them.
> The squirrel *gathered* nuts and *buried* them.

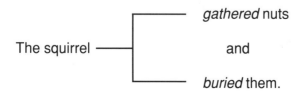

The squirrel    *gathered* nuts
                and
                *buried* them.

**1**

The team *played* very well. The team *won* the game.
The team *played* very well and *won* the game.

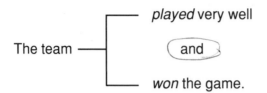

The team ——— *played* very well

and

*won* the game.

### ■ 11 Sentences with Compound Subjects *and* Compound Predicates

It is possible to write simple sentences that have two or more important words in the subject. The same sentence may also have two or more important verbs in the predicate. When this happens, we have a simple sentence with a **compound subject** and a **compound predicate**.

You can see this in the next two examples. The complete subject is separated from the complete predicate by a short vertical line. The two most important words in the compound subject are printed in boldface, and the two most important words in the compound predicate are printed in italics.

**Dad** and **I** | *drove* to the store and *got* some ice cream.

**Susan** and **Mary** | *studied* hard and *passed* the test.

The following illustrations show how the **compound subject** and the **compound predicate** are formed in these two simple sentences.

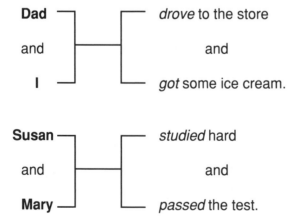

**Dad** —— *drove* to the store

and      and

**I** —— *got* some ice cream.

**Susan** —— *studied* hard

and      and

**Mary** —— *passed* the test.

# Compound Sentences

You know that you can combine important words to form a *compound subject* or a *compound predicate* in a single sentence. Now we will see how to combine two sentences into one. Look at the following simple sentences, which express ideas that are related to each other:

The wind blew very hard. The rain fell in buckets.

We can make sure that the reader sees the relationship between these sentences if we write them this way:

The **wind** *blew* very hard, and the **rain** *fell* in buckets.

Now we have one sentence that contains two parts. Each part has its own subject (in boldface) and verb (in italics). This is called a **compound sentence**.

---

* A **compound sentence** contains two or more simple sentences.
* These simple sentences are connected by a word such as *and*, *or*, or *but*.
* Most of the time a **comma** (,) is used at the end of the first part of the compound sentence just before the connecting word.
* A compound sentence expresses two or more *complete thoughts* that belong together.

*and*
*or*
*but*

---

■ **1m** **Using Compound Sentences to Show Relationships**

The next two simple sentences also express thoughts that are clearly related to each other.

Space flight is interesting. I know a lot about it.

These simple sentences can be joined to form one compound sentence. Notice again that each part of the compound sentence *contains its own subject and verb*.

**1**

**Space flight** *is* interesting, and **I** *know* a lot about it.

Now we will write this sentence again to show how it is constructed. A short vertical line is placed between the subject and predicate in each part of the compound sentence. The comma is used at the end of the first simple sentence, and the word *and* joins these two simple sentences into one compound sentence.

Space flight | is interesting,    and    I | know a lot about it.

The subject of the first part of the sentence is *space flight*, and the subject of the second part is *I*. Many compound sentences have completely different subjects and verbs in each part. However, some compound sentences may use a noun as the subject in the first part and then use a pronoun to take the place of that noun in the second part.

My **friends** *went* to Arizona, and **they** *saw* the Grand Canyon.

Here the subject of the first part of the sentence is *my friends*. In the second part, the subject is the pronoun *they*, which refers to *my friends*. This is still a compound sentence because the second part does contain a subject as well as a verb.

There is another way we can combine the thoughts in this sentence. We can use only the subject *friends* and then follow it with a compound predicate. The subject *they* is not needed.

My **friends** *went* to Arizona and *saw* the Grand Canyon.

You see that there are two ways to combine thoughts. You can choose the type of sentence structure that best expresses what you want to say.

The following examples are compound sentences written by students your age. The two parts of each sentence are joined by the word *and* to show that the ideas are related.

Some houses collapsed, and the church was a wreck.

I ride my horse to the pasture, and then I ride her back and give her carrots and oats.

The bay doors opened, and the starship landed on the floor.

The space invaders demolished some parts of the planet, and the humans declared war on them.

## ■ 1n    Using Compound Sentences to Show Contrast or Choice

Some compound sentences show that there is a **contrast** between the two parts of the sentence. The ideas are related, but the second part of the sentence expresses an idea that is different from the first. The comma and the word *but* are used in compound sentences that show contrast between the two parts.

I thought he was from Chicago, but I wasn't sure.

Sometimes my dreams don't come true, but sometimes they do.

The spaceships turned to get away, but two of them were lost.

The display was attractive, but nobody bought anything.

Each of these compound sentences contains two simple sentences, and each simple sentence has its own subject and predicate. You can see this when we mark off the two parts of the last sentence in the examples you just saw:

The display | was attractive,    but    nobody | bought anything.

There is another word that can be used to join simple sentences into a compound sentence. This is the word *or*, which shows that there is a **choice** offered by the two parts of the sentence. The comma is placed before the word *or*.

We can go to a movie, or we can stay home.

We can stand here and freeze, or we can go in and get warm.

Do you want some pizza, or would you prefer a hot dog?

You can ride with us, or you can wait for a taxi.

The last sentence is written again here to show how the two parts are constructed:

You | can ride with us,    or    you | can wait for a taxi.

**1**

Remember these important points when you write compound sentences:

---

- Use a **comma** at the end of the first part to show the reader that the sentence is not yet complete.
- Use words such as *and*, *or*, or *but* to show the reader that the two parts of the compound sentence are related.
- Be sure that each part of the compound sentence contains its own **subject** and **predicate**.
- Use a **period**, a **question mark**, or an **exclamation mark** at the end of the entire sentence.

---

# Parts of Speech

Throughout this chapter we have talked about *nouns*, *pronouns*, and *verbs*. These terms identify three of the most important kinds of words we use in writing sentences. There are other types of words in addition to these three. Each type of word is called a **part of speech**.

The Parts of Speech are the categories into which words are grouped. They allow us to name the way in which words are *used* in sentences. The most important parts of speech are these:

**noun**

**pronoun**

**verb**

**adjective**

**adverb**

**preposition**

**conjunction**

There is one other type of word called the *interjection* which is often considered another part of speech. Interjections are words such as *Wow!,* *Ouch!,* and *Phooey!* The interjection is of limited importance and does not affect the way sentences are constructed.

Most of the words in any dictionary are nouns, verbs, adjectives, or adverbs. There are hundreds of thousands of these *vocabulary words*, and they allow us to talk about a wide variety of subjects. There are not many pronouns, but they are used very often. There are also only a few prepositions and conjunctions, but they are extremely important. These two parts of speech are known as *function words* or *structure words* because they show relationships among vocabulary words and allow us to construct an enormous variety of sentence patterns.

In the following chapters you will see that many words can serve as different parts of speech. In the English language, words play different roles depending on their location in the sentence. For example, the word *play* is used as a **verb** in this sentence:

We **play** baseball when the weather is good.

In the next sentence, the word *play* is used as a **noun**:

The shortstop made a great **play** and saved the game.

In still another sentence the word *play* is also a noun, but it has a meaning that is different from the one you just saw.

I saw a **play** in the school auditorium yesterday.

Although it is important to be able to recognize the various parts of speech, it is even more important to know how they work together to form clear sentences. Remember that the parts of speech are the names that tell how words are *used* in sentences.

It is not enough simply to put labels on words. It is far more important to know how the various parts of speech relate to each other and how they can be grouped into patterns that allow you to say what you want to say. These are the things we will talk about in this book.

**1**

# *Check Your Understanding*

### Sentences
*Answers begin on p. 263*

**1.** The following **declarative** and **interrogative** sentences contain mistakes. Correct the errors in punctuation.

1. is this the one you're looking for
2. my little sister is five and my brother is seven
3. where did you leave all the stuff I gave you
4. my family is going on a trip to Fresno and Los Angeles
5. are these the only raccoons you have

**2.** Add the necessary capital letters and end punctuation so that these **imperative** and **exclamatory** sentences will be correct.

1. watch out for the thin ice
2. please don't make so much noise
3. i couldn't believe he made that catch
4. just leave the packages on the table
5. that was the most fun i ever had

**3.** Change these sentences so that each question becomes a statement and each statement becomes a question. You can do this by changing the order of the subject and predicate in each sentence. Also change the end punctuation.

1. Are they going to leave tomorrow?
2. He is one of the best students in class.
3. Is this a good book about space travel?
4. They have already gone back home.
5. Should I write a story about a monster from space?

# *Check Your Understanding*

*is*
*are*
*was*
*have*

## Subjects and Predicates

**1.** Draw a short line between the **complete subject** and the **complete predicate** in each sentence. Then underline the *simple subject* and the *simple predicate*. Here is an example:

> The <u>students</u> in my class | <u>took</u> a trip to the museum.

    1. Yesterday we drove up to see my grandparents.
    2. The players on my team are all very good.
    3. One day I met a purple space creature on the bus.
    4. Finally they reached the end of their journey.
    5. The first question was the most difficult of all.

**2.** Indicate whether each of these sentences has a **compound subject** *or* a **compound predicate**. Then write the words that make up each subject or predicate. Here is an example:

> Last week Dad and I went to see a ball game.
> Compound subject: Dad and I

    1. In the summer I swim a lot and play baseball every day.
    2. My friends and I are going camping this summer
    3. Snakes and lizards are not my favorite animals.
    4. My dog ran away from me and chased a squirrel.
    5. Susan and Ellen went to the circus together.

**3.** Here are pairs of short sentences. Use a **compound subject** or a **compound predicate** to combine each pair of sentences into one sentence. Here is an example.

> I called him three times. I finally got an answer.
> I called him three times and finally got an answer.

    1. We went to New York. We saw the Statue of Liberty.
    2. Evan plays on the team. I play on the team.
    3. They stood at the window. They watched the storm raging.
    4. Kate went to the movies. Her friend went to the movies.
    5. My friend called. She asked me to come to her house.

# *Check Your Understanding*

## Simple and Compound Sentences

1. In these **compound sentences**, draw a short line between the subject and predicate of **each part** of the sentence. Here is an example:

> The elephants | performed, and then the clowns | came out.

1. Kay wanted to see a movie, but she played soccer instead.
2. We wandered through the woods, and we saw some chipmunks.
3. Both boys play football, and they are very good.
4. Some people like the mountains, but others prefer the beach.
5. They arrived last Monday, and they stayed for three days.

2. Here are some pairs of simple sentences. Rewrite each example so that it forms a compound sentence. Use *and* or *but* to connect the two parts of the compound sentence. Here is an example:

> I looked all over the place. I couldn't find anything.
> I looked all over the place, but I couldn't find anything.

1. Fred is really a cat. He acts like a person.
2. Ellen liked the book. I liked it, too.
3. I wanted to go bowling. We went to a movie instead.
4. He was not very big. He played football anyway.
5. My family went to California. We had a good time.

3. Here are some examples that could be compound sentences if they were written correctly. Make the necessary changes so that each example becomes a good compound sentence.

1. He fell down at the beginning of the race. But he still won.
2. We ran down the stairs. And we raced out the door.
3. They went to New York. They visited their relatives.
4. The trip was fun. But I was glad when it was over.
5. We can stay a little longer. Or we can leave now.

# 2

# Nouns

You already know that the **noun** is one of the most important and frequently used parts of speech.

> • **Nouns** are words that name people, places, or things.

In the following sentences, the nouns are written in boldface.

My **brother** put his **bicycle** in the **garage**.

The **beauty** of this **flower** is remarkable.

The **warmth** of the **fire** was most welcome.

## ■ 2 a    Types of Nouns

There are several kinds of nouns in the sentences you just read. Some of them go beyond the usual groupings of *people*, *places*, or *things*. Here are some other categories of nouns:

**PERSON:** woman, man, girl, boy, uncle, aunt, grandmother, grandfather, friend, neighbor, teacher, singer, swimmer, author, doctor

**PLACE:** house, porch, garage, attic, school, city, town, village, state, country, neighborhood, airport

**THING:** book, coat, car, tree, newspaper, window, table, chair, bed, radio, sofa, bicycle, skateboard

**ANIMAL:** bird, fish, dog, cat, elephant, zebra, mouse

**GROUP:** class, team, club, troop, audience, herd, pack

**ACTION:** a jump, a touch, laughter, a race, a fall

**EVENT:** journey, vacation, trip, party, meeting, test

**TIME:** second, minute, hour, day, week, month, year, century, morning, noon, night, dawn, dusk, evening, midnight

**IDEA or FEELING or QUALITY:** truth, beauty, fear, joy, honor, justice, happiness, democracy, loneliness

**2**

### ■  2 b    Collective Nouns

Many nouns name individual people or things, but a number of nouns name *groups* of people or animals or things. These are called **collective nouns**.

> • **Collective nouns** name a large number or collection of individual people or things.

Here are some sentences using collective nouns. You can see that no individual member of any group is named.

A **herd** of elephants wandered across the plain.

All the players on the **team** tried very hard to win.

Everyone in my **class** waited for the bell to ring.

All the people in the **audience** were applauding.

### ■  2 c    Concrete Nouns and Abstract Nouns

Look at the nouns in boldface in this sentence.

The first **story** in this **book** is filled with **humor** as well as **sadness**.

The first two words in boldface are **concrete nouns**, while the other two words are **abstract nouns**.

> • **Concrete nouns** name things that you can *see* or *touch*. Here the word *concrete* means "real" and "specific."
> • **Abstract nouns** name ideas, emotions, or qualities that cannot be seen or touched.

The words in the following list show the difference between these two types of nouns:

| Concrete | Abstract |
|----------|----------|
| house | honor |
| tree | truth |
| boat | beauty |
| table | fear |
| dog | joy |
| chair | wisdom |

## ■ 2 d    Base Words

Before going on, we should introduce a term that will be used throughout this book. The term is **base word**.

> • A **base word** is a complete word that can stand by itself. The base form gives the essential meaning of the word. It gives the spelling of the word before any endings are added or other changes are made.

As you will soon see, base words can be changed by the addition of various endings. They can also be combined with other words or word parts to create new words.

Most of the nouns we have seen so far have been base words: *dog, story, bird,* and *journey*, for example. Now we will see how the base form of these nouns can be used in different ways.

## ■ 2 e    Compound Nouns

Look at the nouns in boldface in this sentence:

My **homework** and my **notebook** are in my **backpack**, wherever that is.

These nouns are **compound words**.

> • **Compound words** are made up of two or more individual words. Often these words are nouns in their base forms. You can often tell the meaning of the compound word by looking at the individual words.

**2**

- **Closed compounds** join shorter words without any break between them.

| | | |
|---|---|---|
| football | bedroom | skateboard |
| haircut | baseball | rattlesnake |
| toothbrush | mailbox | grandfather |
| wastebasket | snowstorm | grandmother |
| wheelchair | fingerprint | basketball |

- **Hyphenated compounds** connect words with a short dash called a **hyphen** (-).

| | |
|---|---|
| baby-sitter | great-grandmother |
| front-runner | great-grandfather |
| by-product | mother-in-law |
| runner-up | father-in-law |
| hide-and-seek | merry-go-round |

- **Open compounds** are written as separate words. We recognize that the words work together to create a new term which goes beyond the meaning of each individual word.

| | |
|---|---|
| hot dog | post office |
| high school | sewing machine |
| swimming pool | comic strip |
| ice cream | gas station |
| fire engine | city hall |
| hang glider | science fiction |

# Singular Nouns and Plural Nouns

- **Singular nouns** name only *one* person or place or thing.
- **Plural nouns** name *more than one* person or place or thing.

When we want to name more than one person or thing, we change the singular noun by adding **inflections**.

- **Inflections** are alterations which show that there has been a change in the way a word is used.
- Nouns are inflected to show a change in *number*, from singular to plural.
- Usually the inflection involves a letter or two letters added to the end of a base word (*book*, *books*; *glass*, *glasses*).
- Occasionally, inflections change the vowel or other letters in the base word (*man*, *men*; *person*, *people*).

■ **2 f    Forming the Plural by Adding *s***

- With most nouns, the inflection *s* is added to the end of the base word to change from singular to plural.

This is the case with nouns that end with *two consonants* or with a *vowel* followed by a *consonant*. We add the final *s* to nouns such as *worker* and *doctor* that end with -*er* or -*or,* and we also add *s* to nouns that end with silent *e*.

| | |
|---|---|
| book, books | student, students |
| grape, grapes | occasion, occasions |
| dime, dimes | stove, stoves |
| rope, ropes | miracle, miracles |
| crumb, crumbs | nation, nations |
| plant, plants | pond, ponds |
| runner, runners | doctor, doctors |

When compound nouns are written as one word, add *s* to the end of the final word.

textbook**s**, snowshoe**s**, backpack**s**

When compound nouns are joined by a hyphen or are written as separate words, add *s* to the end of the most important word.

high school**s**, mother**s**-in-law

**2**

### ■ 2 g    Forming the Plural by Adding *es*

Some nouns add the inflection *es* instead of *s* to the end of the base word to form the plural.

> • The inflection *es* is added to nouns that end with the sounds /s/, /sh/, /ch/, /ks/, or /z/ in the singular.

When *es* is added to a base word, it forms a separate syllable. Here are some examples of nouns that use the inflection *es* to form the plural:

| Ending of base word | Words that add *es* to form the plural | |
|---|---|---|
| /s/*s*, *ss* | bus, buses | class, classes |
| /sh/*sh* | brush, brushes | crash, crashes |
| /ch/*ch*, *tch* | lunch, lunches | watch, watches |
| /ks/*x* | box, boxes | tax, taxes |
| /z/*z*, *zz* | whiz, whizzes | buzz, buzzes |

Compound nouns that are written as one word also add *es* to the final word when it ends with the letters shown above.

lunchbox**es**    toothbrush**es**

### ■ 2 h    Forming the Plural in Nouns Ending with *y* and *ie*

• When a noun ends with a **vowel** followed by the letter *y*, add *s* to form the plural. Do the same with nouns that end with *ie*.

| | |
|---|---|
| boy, boys | toy, toys |
| day, days | tray, trays |
| key, keys | monkey, monkeys |
| turkey, turkeys | chimney, chimneys |
| valley, valleys | journey, journeys |
| | |
| pie, pies | tie, ties |
| movie, movies | prairie, prairies |
| collie, collies | calorie, calories |

- When a noun ends with a **consonant** followed by *y*, change the final *y* to *i* and add *es* to form the plural.

| | |
|---|---|
| fly, flies | lullaby, lullabies |
| baby, babies | lady, ladies |
| puppy, puppies | berry, berries |

■ **2 i** **Forming the Plural in Nouns Ending with *f*, *fe*, and *ff***

- A number of nouns ending with *f* or *fe* change the *f* to *v* and add *es* to form the plural.

| | |
|---|---|
| leaf, leaves | shelf, shelves |
| wolf, wolves | calf, calves |
| loaf, loaves | hoof, hooves |
| life, lives | knife, knives |

- Other words that end with a **vowel** followed by *f* or *ff* often add *s* to form the plural.

| | |
|---|---|
| cliff, cliffs | bluff, bluffs |
| staff, staffs | chef, chefs |
| roof, roofs | sheriff, sheriffs |
| chief, chiefs | giraffe, giraffes |

■ **2 j** **Forming the Plural in Nouns Ending with *o***

- Nouns that end with the letter *o* preceded by a **vowel** add only *s* to form the plural.

| | | |
|---|---|---|
| radio, radios | studio, studios | ratio, ratios |
| video, videos | stereo, stereos | rodeo, rodeos |

- Nouns that end with the letter *o* preceded by a **consonant** often add *es* to form the plural.

| | | |
|---|---|---|
| hero, heroes | echo, echoes | potato, potatoes |
| veto, vetoes | tomato, tomatoes | volcano, volcanoes |

- A few words that end with *o* preceded by a consonant add only *s* to form the plural. Many of these are words taken into English from other languages such as Italian.

| | | |
|---|---|---|
| solo, solos | piano, pianos | alto, altos |
| dynamo, dynamos | kimono, kimonos | auto, autos |

■ **2 k    Irregular Plural Forms**

A few plural nouns do not simply add an inflection to the end of the singular form. In these words the inflection often affects the vowel and thus changes the pronunciation of the entire word. These are called **irregular plural forms** because they do not follow the patterns we have just seen for adding *s* or *es* to form the plural. Here are some of the most frequently used irregular plural nouns:

| | |
|---|---|
| man, men | woman, women |
| foot, feet | tooth, teeth |
| person, people | child, children |
| goose, geese | mouse, mice |

When you use these words to write compound nouns, be sure to use the correct spelling of these irregular plural forms.

| | |
|---|---|
| policeman, policemen | policewoman, policewomen |
| salesperson, salespeople | schoolchild, schoolchildren |

■ **2 l    Nouns That Are the Same in Singular and Plural**

A few nouns do not change their spelling at all in the singular and plural forms. The nouns you are most likely to use are *fish*, *deer*, *moose*, and *sheep*. Dictionaries often list *fishes* as a possible plural for *fish*.

■ **2 m    Singular Nouns That End with *s***

A few nouns end with *s* and look as though they might be plural. In fact, these nouns are singular and should be used with a verb that is also singular. Verbs will be discussed in Chapter 4 of this book. For now, we will mention a few of these nouns and show how some of them may be used in sentences.

| | |
|---|---|
| news | physics |
| politics | economics |
| measles | civics |

The *news* is much better today than it was yesterday.

*Measles* can be a serious disease.

*Physics* is the scientific study of matter and energy.

## ■ 2 n    Nouns That Are Always Plural

A few nouns exist *only* in the plural. There is no singular form for these words. Notice that most of these words name things that consist of two parts.

| | |
|---|---|
| scissors | pants |
| shorts | trousers |
| pliers | glasses |
| scales | goods |

These *scissors* are very dull.

Those *scales* were not very accurate.

The *pliers* are bent out of shape.

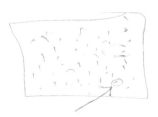

Your orange *trousers* were hanging in the closet.

# Common Nouns and Proper Nouns

So far we have seen nouns that could be used to name *any* person or place or any of the other categories we listed. These are called **common nouns.**

> • **Common nouns** can apply to *anyone* or to *anything*. They name only general categories: *boy, girl, dog, city, state*.

When we want to indicate exactly which person or place or thing we are talking about, we use a **proper noun**.

> • **Proper nouns** name *specific* people or places or things: *Edward, Susan, Rover, Dallas, Texas*.
> • Proper nouns are always capitalized.

The names of people are always proper nouns, as are the names of cities, states, and countries. Important geographical features (lakes, rivers, oceans, mountains) are proper nouns. All the days and months are also proper nouns.

The following list shows a few common nouns followed by examples of proper nouns that name specific people or things.

| Common Nouns | Proper Nouns |
| --- | --- |
| president | George Washington, Abraham Lincoln |
| writer | Mark Twain, Edgar Allan Poe |
| artist | Claude Monet, Pablo Picasso |
| building | Empire State Building, The White House |
| city | San Francisco, Atlanta |
| state | Montana, Florida |
| country | Germany, India |
| month | July, September |
| day | Monday, Wednesday |
| river | Mississippi River, Amazon River |
| lake | Lake Erie, Lake Michigan |
| ocean | Atlantic Ocean, Indian Ocean |
| holiday | New Year's Day, Fourth of July |
| mountain | Mount Everest, Mount McKinley |
| continent | Asia, Africa |

■ **2 o    Using Common and Proper Nouns in Sentences**

The following sentences contain both common nouns and proper nouns. Both types of noun are printed in boldface. The proper nouns are the words that are capitalized.

**Chicago** is a large **city** in **Illinois**.

**Edward** and **Tom** are my best **friends**.

**Britain** and **France** are **countries** in **Europe**.

We went to **Denver** last **August** and stayed for a **week**.

**George Washington** was the first **president** of the **United States**.

# Possessive Nouns

A **possessive noun** shows that something *belongs* to someone.

Harry**'s** nose is red.

The teachers' meetings lasted all day.

Special inflections are used at the end of nouns to show possession.

■ **2 p**    **Singular Possessive Nouns**

> - **Singular possessive nouns** are usually formed by adding an *apostrophe* (') and *s* to the base word.
> - This **inflection** ('s) is used most of the time to form singular possessive nouns.

Is this your **dog's** collar?

The **child's** parents came to our house.

Each **class's** teacher was in the meeting.

There is one special category of singular nouns that can be handled differently.

> - If a singular noun ends with *s* and contains *more than one syllable*, then you may add *only* an apostrophe to show possession. Usually this is done to avoid too many /s/ sounds, especially if the following word also begins with the /s/ sound.

The jury did not believe the **witness'** story.          *witness's*

The **actress'** singing was unusual.

You will be correct, however, if you add **'s** to the end of any *singular* noun, no matter what the final letter is.

**2**

The **actress's** latest movie was a hit.

The **hostess's** party was a great success.

■ **2 q    Plural Possessive Nouns**

Most plural nouns already end with *s* or *es*.

> • Plural nouns that end with *s* or *es* add only an **apostrophe (')** to show possession.
> • This **inflection (')** is used most of the time to form plural possessive nouns.

These books were damaged in the storm. All the **books'** covers have been ruined.

The students left their coats in the closet. Most of the **students'** coats were dripping wet.

Those bushes need to be trimmed. All the **bushes'** branches are too long.

I have two favorite actresses. Both **actresses'** movies were on TV last night.

We have seen **irregular plural nouns** that do not add *s* or *es* to form the plural: *men, women, children, people,* for example.

> • Add *apostrophe* and *s* (*'s*) to nouns that do *not* end with *s* or *es* in the plural.

The **women's** hats are over there.

Are there many **children's** books in this store?

The **people's** ideas were presented in the meeting.

# Nouns in a Series

Sometimes we use several words of the same type in a **series**.

The tree was filled with **robins**, **cardinals**, and **sparrows**.

> • A **series** is a group of similar or related things that come one after another. A series of words usually contains several words that belong to the same part of speech.

The letters A, B, C, D, E form a series in alphabetical order. The numbers 1, 2, 3, 4, 5 form a series in numerical order. We can also have a series of baseball games, a series of meetings, or a series of words that are all nouns or pronouns or verbs or other parts of speech.

We often use two or more nouns in a series.

> • When there are *only* two nouns in a series, the words are usually joined by *and* or *or*.

In Section **1 j** you saw this use of *and* and *or* when nouns were used as *compound subjects*.

**Monkeys and elephants** are my favorite animals.

**Carlos or Ed** will bring the potato chips.

It is also possible to use *and* or *or* to join two or more nouns at other places within the sentence.

They gave some corn to the **horses and cows**.

Did he lose **his hat or his gloves** at the game?

**2**

### ■ 2 r    Three or More Nouns in a Series

When *more* than two nouns are used in a series, they should be separated so that the reader can make sense of the sentence. See how confusing these sentences are when nouns are not separated:

I didn't want carrots tomatoes spinach broccoli.

Are there enough pens pencils and erasers for everyone?

Now see how much clearer these sentences are when we use commas to separate the words in each series:

I don't want carrots, tomatoes, spinach, or broccoli!

Are there enough pens, pencils, and erasers for everyone?

> • When three or more nouns are used in a series, add a **comma** to separate each noun from the noun that follows it.
> • Use a word such as *and* or *or* before the last noun in the series.

Look at the next sentence, written by a student in the middle grades. You can imagine how confusing it would be if the nouns weren't separated by commas.

To cure a cold you will need some hot sauce, red peppers, green peppers, onions, twenty-five drops of juice, some Coke, Pepsi, grease, salt, pepper, and a banana.

The placement of commas can even affect the meaning of the sentence. Although the next two sentences contain the same words, they have different meanings because commas have been used to organize the words into different groups.

I like chocolate ice cream and pizza.

I like chocolate, ice cream, and pizza.

You can see that it is important to use commas carefully so that words will be grouped as you want them to be.

# *Check Your Understanding*

## Singular and Plural Nouns
*Answers begin on p. 266.*

1. These nouns are written in the singular form. Write each noun in its **plural** form.

   1. mailbox
   2. supply
   3. berry
   4. crutch
   5. apology

   6. territory
   7. ambush
   8. associate
   9. journey
   10. director

2. These nouns are also written in the singular. Write each noun in its **plural** form.

   1. potato
   2. leaf
   3. child
   4. shelf
   5. tomato

   6. radio
   7. cliff
   8. woman
   9. volcano
   10. piano

3. Underline all the nouns you find in each sentence.

   1. The river wound through the canyon to the sea.
   2. All the owls and hawks were hunting for rabbits and mice.
   3. The porch, the roof, and the garage were badly damaged.
   4. Our journey began by car and continued by ship and plane.
   5. Engineers designed a tunnel through the mountain.

**2**

# *Check Your Understanding*

## Common and Proper Nouns; Nouns in a Series

**1.** Underline each common noun once and each proper noun twice.

    1. Holland and Belgium are neighboring countries.

    2. Dolphins and whales are found in the Pacific Ocean.

    3. The continents of Europe and Asia are connected.

    4. Get out the overcoats and snowshoes before winter arrives.

    5. All the plates and glasses are on the shelf.

**2.** Add commas and the word *and* to clarify these sentences containing nouns in a series.

    1. The room was filled with sofas chairs tables lamps.
    2. My brothers sisters friends all came to my party.
    3. Where are my books papers pencils?
    4. The storm blew twigs leaves paper into the yard.
    5. We saw horses elephants clowns acrobats at the circus.

## Possessive Nouns

**1.** Use the possessive forms of each noun in parentheses. Read each sentence carefully to see if the nouns should be singular or plural.

    1. One (car) left front fender was damaged.
    2. Both (plane) pilots were in the air show.
    3. This (knife) blade is not sharp enough to cut the rope.
    4. All three of my (friend) parents were at the meeting.
    5. This brown (bear) paws are extremely large.

**2.** Write the singular possessive and the plural possessive form of each noun listed below. In some cases you must add an inflection and also change the spelling of the noun.

    Example: child - child's, children's

| monkey | holiday | woman | volcano |
| --- | --- | --- | --- |
| person | country | house | journey |

# 3

# Pronouns

In Chapter 2 you saw that **nouns** are words that name people or places or things. A noun is often used as the subject of the sentence.

Look at the following pairs of sentences. Arrows show the relationship between the words written in boldface.

Our **neighbors** left on vacation. **They** are going to Chicago.

**Ellen** is a very good student. **She** likes math and science.

The nouns *neighbors* and *Ellen* are the subjects in the first sentence of each pair. In the second sentence of each pair, these nouns have been replaced by *they* and *she*. These words are **pronouns**.

> • A **pronoun** is a word that takes the place of a noun or nouns. A pronoun can also take the place of any words that are associated with the noun.

The following examples show how individual pronouns can be used in place of groups of words that make up the complete subject of each sentence.

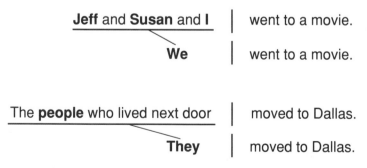

| **Jeff** and **Susan** and **I** | went to a movie. |
| **We** | went to a movie. |

| The **people** who lived next door | moved to Dallas. |
| **They** | moved to Dallas. |

Pronouns are among the most important parts of speech. They are valuable because they allow us to avoid repeating the same nouns over and over.

**3**

# Personal Pronouns

The pronouns we use most often are called **personal pronouns**.

> • **Personal pronouns** are words which usually take the place of nouns that name *people*. Some personal pronouns can take the place of nouns that name *things*.
> • Personal pronouns can refer to the person who is speaking, the person who is spoken to, or the person who is spoken about.

## ■ 3 a  Personal Pronouns Used as Subjects

These are the personal pronouns that can be used as **subjects** in sentences:

|              | SUBJECT PRONOUNS | |
| --- | --- | --- |
|              | **Singular** | **Plural** |
| **First person** | I | we |
| **Second person** | you | you |
| **Third person** | he, she, it | they |

> • Pronouns in the **first person** refer to the person who is **speaking** (*I*, *we*).
> • The pronoun in the **second person** refers to the person who is **spoken to** (*you*).
> • Pronouns in the **third person** refer to the people or things that are **spoken about** (*he, she, it, they*). *He* and *she* refer only to people; *it* refers to things. *They* may refer to either people or things.

*I* and *we* are the only pronouns that can be used as subjects in the first person.

I hope our team will win the game this Saturday.

Kay and I are good friends. **We** go everywhere together.

*You* is the only word that can be used as a subject in the second person, singular or plural.

> I like this very much. **You** may like it, too.

> John and I are leaving now. **You** may come with us.

The following sentences use subject pronouns in the third person. Each pronoun in italics refers to the noun in boldface in the first sentence of each group.

> Evan was not in school yesterday. **He** must be ill.

> I saw Maria yesterday. **She** was going to the mall.

> The TV set is broken. **It** just buzzes and pops.

> My friends are coming over. **They** will be here soon.

> Both umbrellas are broken. **They** won't open at all.

## ■  3 b    Personal Pronouns Used as Objects

In addition to their use as subjects in sentences, personal pronouns can also be used as **objects**.

> • **Object pronouns** are often used to who tell *who* or *what* received the action of the verb.
>
> > I saw **her** at the movies.
> > We met **them** on the playground.
> > He threw **it** in the trash.
>
> • **Object pronouns** are also used after words such as *for*, *with*, and *to*.
>
> > This package is for **him**.
> > They are going with **us** on the trip.
> > I am supposed to give this note to **you**.

**3**

When pronouns are used as objects, most of them have spellings that are different from their spellings as subject pronouns.

OBJECT PRONOUNS

|  | **Singular** | **Plural** |
|---|---|---|
| **First person** | me | us |
| **Second person** | you | you |
| **Third person** | him, her, it | them |

Did you notice that *you* is used as an *object pronoun* as well as a *subject pronoun*? It is the position of *you* in the sentence that is important.

The following sentences show how object pronouns are used:

When I went to a new school, everyone helped **me** get started.
My parents gave some new clothes to **me** for Christmas.
The policeman told **us** to turn left at the next corner.
Fred and I were late, but our friends waited for **us**.
Didn't I see **you** at the game last Saturday?
Will your parents go with **you** on the trip?
Mike said he was there, but I didn't see **him**.
Please give Mike's gloves to **him** when you see **him**.
Kim went to the movies. I saw **her** there.
Will you take Ellen's books back to **her**?
That movie is great. I saw **it** last week.
The room was such a mess that I didn't want to look at **it**.
My friends aren't here now, but I saw **them** yesterday.
Please give this book to Ed and Sarah when you see **them**.

### ■ 3 c    The Antecedent of the Pronoun

Sentences often begin with the pronoun *I*, and everyone understands that this pronoun refers to the person who is writing. Sometimes, though, the writer may give his or her name and then continue with the pronoun *I*.

Hi! My name is *Maria*, and **I** am a student in the fifth grade. **I** like history and spelling, and **I** also play softball after school. **I** like my teacher very much.

This student first gives her name: *Maria*. We know that the pronoun *I* always refers to *Maria*. This means that the proper noun *Maria* is the **antecedent** of the pronoun *I*.

- The word *antecedent* means "something that is placed in front of something else" or "something that occurs before another event."
- In language, the **antecedent** is a noun or group of words to which a pronoun refers. It is the noun or group of words that is replaced by the pronoun.

When we use pronouns, it is important for the antecedent to be clear. If a pronoun is going to take the place of a noun, then the reader must be able to tell what that noun is. In the following sentences, the arrows point from each pronoun (printed in boldface) back to its antecedent (printed in italics).

*Ken and I* left early, and **we** got there in plenty of time.

*Susan* is my friend. **She** is in my class at school.

*My bike* is not working. I think **it** needs new brakes.

*My friends* liked that movie. **They** thought it was great.

In these four examples, all the pronouns were used as **subjects**. It is also important to make the antecedent clear when we use pronouns as **objects**. In Section **3b** you saw sentences that used object pronouns. A few of these sentences are repeated here, with each **object pronoun** again printed in boldface. The *antecedent* of each pronoun is printed in italics.

When *I* went to a new school, everyone helped **me** get started.

*We* weren't sure which way to go. Then someone told **us** to turn left at the next corner.

Please give *Mike's* gloves to **him** when you see **him**.

*Kim* went to the movies. I saw **her** there.

The *movie* is great. I saw **it** last week.

My *friends* aren't here now, but I saw **them** yesterday.

**3**

### ■ 3 d    Showing How Pronouns Relate to Antecedents

Sometimes a sentence may contain more than one word that could be the antecedent of a pronoun. Look at the problems that appear in this sentence:

> **Ed** stayed after school while his friend **Bill** practiced basketball. *His* mom asked *him* why he was late.

*Whose* mom asked *him* why he was late? Does the word *him* refer to Ed or Bill? We can't find the antecedent because the wording is not clear. We need to specify *who* was asked about being late. Then the pronoun *him* will have a clear antecedent.

> **Ed** stayed after school while his friend **Bill** practiced basketball. **Ed's** mom asked *him* why he was late.

Here is another sentence in which the antecedent is not clear:

> The car was parked too close to the truck. They scraped together when *it* tried to move away.

You can see that the pronoun *they* refers to the car *and* the truck, but what does the pronoun *it* refer to in the second sentence? Did the car or the truck move away? Again, it is impossible to tell. You can make the sentences clear by indicating which vehicle actually moved.

> The car was parked too close to the truck. They scraped together when the truck tried to move away.

If more than one word can be the antecedent of a pronoun, then it is better to repeat the noun so that the meaning is clear.

It will help to remember that the pronouns *he, she, him, her,* and *it* refer to an antecedent that is **singular**. This means that sentences such as the following are clear because these singular pronouns can refer to only one antecedent.

> *Mary* and the students in her class went on a trip. **She** showed them where **her** father worked.

**She** and **her** refer only to *Mary* (singular), not to *the students in her class* (plural). Now look at this slight change in the second sentence:

Mary and the students in her class went on a trip. They went to see where **her** father worked.

The plural pronoun *they* in the second sentence refers to *Mary and the students in her class*. The singular pronoun *her* still refers only to Mary.

### ■ 3 e    Using Subject and Object Pronouns with Nouns

Look at this sentence. Can you tell exactly who is included in the subject?

**We** helped clear the vacant lot.

You know that it must have been the writer and at least one other person because the subject is the plural pronoun *we*. However, we still don't know who else was involved.

Does this sentence make things any clearer?

**Students** helped clear the vacant lot.

Now we know that the subject is *students*, but we don't know if the writer was one of them or not. Here is how the writer can show that he or she was one of the people involved:

**We students** helped clear the vacant lot.

When you use this combination of a pronoun and a noun in the subject, be sure to use the **subject pronoun** *we*. This is the only pronoun that can be used in this combination to form the subject of the sentence. Just remember that you would use *we* as the subject by itself, so you use *we* plus a plural noun when they are combined to form the subject.

Now look at the next sentence:

The neighbors thanked **us students** for helping them.

Here the pronoun *us* is used as the **object**, and it is again combined with the noun *students*. The first person plural pronoun is used in its object form, *us*, because it comes after the verb and tells who was thanked. The noun *students* makes it even more specific.

You would not write the following sentence, would you?

The neighbors thanked **we** for helping them,

This is obviously wrong because *we* is a subject pronoun. For that reason, you would not write: "The neighbors thanked *we students* for helping them." When the plural pronoun is combined with a plural noun to form the object of a sentence, the pronoun should be used in the object form, *us*.

As you have seen, the pronoun *you* can be subject or object, singular or plural. This means that you can write sentences such as these which combine *you* with plural nouns:

*You students* did a good job. (subject)

I want to thank *you students* for doing a good job. (object)

> • Only the plural pronouns **we**, **you**, and **us** can be used in combination with plural nouns. Do not let the presence of the noun confuse you. Always use **we** as the *subject* and **us** as the *object*. **You** can be used in either situation.

You can always be sure that sentences are correct if you write them with the pronoun alone before you add the noun. Here is another example that combines the **subject pronoun** *we* with a noun:

**We** drew pictures for the newspaper.
**Artists** drew pictures for the newspaper.

**We artists** drew pictures for the newspaper.

This example combines the **object pronoun** with a noun:

They gave a prize to **us** for the newspaper article.
They gave a prize to the **writers** for the newspaper article.

They gave a prize to **us writers** for the newspaper article.

## ■ 3 f    Pronouns in Compound Subjects and Objects

Be careful when you use the subject pronouns *I*, *he*, *she* and the object pronouns *me*, *him*, *her*. This is especially important when you have two words in the subject or two words as objects in the predicate. (You may want to look back at Section **1j** for information on *compound subjects* and at Section **1k** for information on *compound predicates*.) If you think about *how* these word are used, you will avoid mistakes.

Here is a sentence that appears to have a compound subject:

**Him and me** watched for the school bus.

As it stands, the compound subject is *him and me*. You can see what is wrong if you construct separate sentences using each pronoun individually as the subject.

**Him** watched for the school bus.

**Me** watched for the school bus.

You wouldn't write or speak this way. You would correct these sentences like this:

**He** watched for the school bus.

**I** watched for the school bus.

You can combine the two individual subject pronouns using the word *and*. The fact that there are two pronouns does not change the need to use **subject pronouns** in the subject part of the sentence.

**He and I** watched for the school bus.

Here is another sentence with an incorrect pronoun in the **compound object** that follows the word *to*:

They gave it to **Frances and I**.

There is nothing wrong with saying "They gave it to *Frances*," but you wouldn't say "They gave it to *I*." Again, don't be fooled by the fact that the object contains two words.

They gave it to Frances and **me**.

What is wrong in the next sentence?

**Me and John** went to the ball game yesterday.

**3**

This sentence begins with *me*, which is an object pronoun. You would not say "Me went to the ball game yesterday," so you would not say "Me and John" in a compound subject. Here is how this sentence can be corrected using the subject pronoun *I:*

John and **I** went to the ball game yesterday.

Look at this incorrect sentence:

We looked for **she and Kim** at the mall.

Again, you can separate this into two short sentences to see what is wrong with the pronoun.

We looked for **she** at the mall.

We looked for **Kim** at the mall.

The object pronoun *her* is needed in the first sentence: "We looked for *her*." Also remember that a person's name is usually given before a pronoun. We can combine the two words in the compound object and write this sentence correctly by using the object pronoun:

We looked for **Kim and her** at the mall.

# Possessive Pronouns

In Sections **2p** and **2q** you saw that **possessive nouns** can be used to show that something belongs to someone. *Singular* nouns usually add an **apostrophe** and the letter *s* (*'s*) to form the possessive. *Plural* nouns ending with *s* usually added only the apostrophe in the possessive.

The road**'s** surface was slick and dangerous.

All the girls' coats were hanging in the closet.

It is also possible to use **possessive pronouns**. These pronouns do *not* simply add an inflection to a base word, as nouns did.

## ■ 3 g    Possessive Pronouns Used with Nouns

When we want to write **possessive pronouns**, we use a special form of the pronoun in the first, second, and third person. These spellings are different from the subject pronouns you saw in Section **3a** and the object pronouns you saw in Section **3b**. Here are the personal pronouns that are placed directly before nouns to show possession:

**POSSESSIVE PRONOUNS
USED WITH NOUNS**

|  | Singular | Plural |
|---|---|---|
| **First person** | my | our |
| **Second person** | your | your |
| **Third person** | his, her, its | their |

The following sentences show how these possessive pronouns are used:

This book belongs to me. This is **my** book.

We bought a lawn mower. Here is **our** new mower.

Doesn't this book belong to you? Isn't it **your** book?

That coat belongs to John. It is **his** coat.

Maria can't find **her** homework.

The tree blew down and **its** limbs damaged the roof.

All of our neighbors mowed **their** lawns on Saturday.

## ■ 3 h    Possessive Pronouns That Stand Alone

There are other possessive pronouns that can stand alone. These pronouns do *not* have to be used directly before a noun.

**POSSESSIVE PRONOUNS
THAT STAND ALONE**

|  | Singular | Plural |
|---|---|---|
| **First person** | mine | ours |
| **Second person** | yours | yours |
| **Third person** | his, hers, its | theirs |

**3**

The first person singular changes from *my* to *mine*. Most of the other pronouns in this group add the letter *s* to the forms you saw in Section **3g**. Only *his* and *its* remain the same whether they are used alone or before nouns. It is unlikely that you will use the third person pronoun (*its*) alone; this word is more often used directly before a noun. The next two sentences show how *his* can be used before a noun or alone.

This is *his* book. This book is *his*.

The next group of sentences shows how these possessive pronouns can be used. The first sentence in each pair lets you know what is being discussed. Then the second sentence of each pair uses a possessive pronoun. When you use these pronouns that can stand alone, it is especially important for the antecedent to be clear.

*I* got a new coat yesterday. This coat is **mine**.

Do these gloves belong to *you*? Are these gloves **yours**?

*He* won the contest. That prize is **his**.

*She* bought a new hat. This hat is **hers**.

*We* just got a new car. This car is **ours**.

*They* won the game. That trophy is **theirs**.

## ■ 3 i Possessive Pronouns and Their Antecedents

In the next sentences you can see that several possessive pronouns can be used to refer to the same antecedent.

**Our game** is on Friday. **Your game** is tomorrow, and **their game** is next week.

**Our game** is on Friday. **Yours** is tomorrow, and **theirs** is next week.

In both sets of sentences, all the pronouns refer to the *game* that is mentioned at the beginning. It is not necessary to keep mentioning *your game* and *their game* because you can use the possessive pronouns *yours* and *theirs* to refer to the antecedent, *game*.

Possessive pronouns **never** contain an apostrophe, as possessive nouns do. This will help you remember that *its* is always a possessive pronoun.

The car crashed when **its** brakes failed.

This bike is rusty and **its** wheels are bent.

Be careful not to confuse the possessive pronoun *its* with the word *it's*, which is a *contraction* formed by combining the words *it is*.

This lawn mower is worn out. **Its** blade is rusty and **its** motor is broken. **It's** not going to start, and **it's** probably too old to repair. (*It is* not going to start, and *it is* probably too old to repair.)

In Section **4n** you will find more information on contractions that involve a pronoun and a shortened form of a verb.

# Using *who, whom,* and *whose*

The pronouns *who, whom,* and *whose* must be used carefully. It is not difficult to know which pronoun to use if you remember what has been said about *subject pronouns, object pronouns,* and *possessive pronouns.*

■ **3 j    Using *who* Correctly**

> • *Who* is always used as the **subject** of the sentence. It can be used in the singular or in the plural. It often appears as the first word in a question.

These sentences show how the pronoun *who* can be used:

**Who** was on the phone?

**Who** won the game?

**Who** knows the answer to that question?

If you want to be sure you are using *who* correctly, then think about the type of pronoun that would be used to *answer* these questions.

**Who** was on the phone?  **She** was on the phone.

**Who** won the game?  **They** won the game.

Each answer uses a **subject pronoun**, so the question should also use the subject pronoun *who*. *Who* was used in the singular (to refer to *she*) and in the plural (to refer to *they*).

Notice how the next two sentences are constructed.

I don't know **who** was on the phone.

I wasn't sure **who** won the game.

Here we have statements rather than questions. The word *who* is still the subject of "Who was on the phone" and "Who won the game". Now these parts of the sentence are preceded by statements that say "I don't know" or "I wasn't sure."

## ■ 3 k     Using *whom* Correctly

> • *Whom* is always used as the **object**. It can also be used as the first word in a question.

Here are some sentences that begin with *whom*. This word is the **object** even though it comes at the beginning of each sentence.

**Whom** did you call?

**Whom** does he work with on that project?

**Whom** are you going to see?

You can be sure you are using *whom* correctly if you think about the type of pronoun that would be used to answer each of these questions.

**Whom** did you call? I called **him**.

**Whom** does he work with on that project? He works with **them**.

**Whom** are you going to see? I am going to see **her**.

The answers use the object pronouns *him*, *them*, and *her*, so the questions should also use the object pronoun *whom*.

You may sometimes hear sentences like those that follow. Even though you know what these sentences mean, there is still a problem with them. In each sentence the subject is in boldface.

Who were **you** speaking to?

Who was the **message** for?

Who did **he** work with?

Each question begins with *who* and ends with the words *to*, *for*, or *with*. These words are called **prepositions**. You will find out more about prepositions in Chapter 7 of this book. For now, remember that a preposition is used to show the relationship between a noun or pronoun and other words in the sentence.

If the subjects of the preceding examples are *you*, *message*, and *he*, how can each sentence begin with *who*, which is a **subject pronoun**? It shouldn't, of course. That is why it is important to be able to recognize the subject and to be sure that pronouns are used correctly. Here the use of the subject pronoun *who* conflicts with the real subject of each sentence.

It would be possible to correct these sentences this way:

**Whom** were you speaking to?

**Whom** was the message for?

**Whom** did he work with?

The arrows point back from the words *to*, *for* and *with* to show that they refer to the object pronoun *whom*. These sentences are acceptable, but the object *whom* is still far away from the preposition at the end of each sentence. Here is still another way these three sentences could be written:

**To whom** were you speaking?

**For whom** was the message sent?

**With whom** did he work?

49

**3**

Each of these sentences begins with a preposition followed by its object, *whom*. There is no more confusion caused by the incorrect subject pronoun *who* at the beginning. When you write sentences using the pronoun *whom*, it is generally best to follow this pattern so that your sentences will always be clear to your readers.

■ **31** **Using *whose* Correctly**

> • *Whose* is a **possessive pronoun**. It is often used to begin a question that asks who owns a certain thing.

These sentences show how this possessive pronoun can be used:

**Whose** books are these?

**Whose** bike is parked outside?

**Whose** pet snake got loose in the classroom?

I don't know **whose** hat this is.

Do you know **whose** parents are coming to visit?

It is important to remember that the spelling *whose* is used for the possessive pronoun. This word is usually followed by a noun. There is another word that sounds the same, but it has a different meaning and use. This is the word *who's*, which is a contraction made up of the pronoun *who* and a shortened form of the verb *is*. Here is how this contraction is used:

**Who's** going to the store? (**Who is** going to the store?)

**Who's** waiting for a ride? (**Who is** waiting for a ride?)

You will find out more about contractions in Section **4n**. For now, remember that *whose* is a possessive pronoun and is usually followed by a noun. The contraction *who's* means *who is*.

**Whose** gloves are these? (**To whom** do these gloves belong?)

**Who's** looking for them? (**Who is** looking for them?)

# Indefinite Pronouns

Look at the words printed in boldface in these sentences:

**Everybody** cheered when our team won the game.

**Nobody** knew what had happened.

**Both** of our parents went to the meeting.

**Somebody** must know where we are.

**Most** of us finished the test on time.

These words are all pronouns, but they do not have specific antecedents. These are called **indefinite pronouns** because they refer to people or things in general, not to any particular person or thing. The meaning of these pronouns is made clear by the general *context*, not by their reference to a specific antecedent.

## ■ 3 m    Pronouns That Refer to *all* or *every*

Some indefinite pronouns are very general and refer to a wide range of people or things. Most of these are singular pronouns and require a singular verb to agree with them. One of these pronouns can be either singular or plural.

| Singular | Singular or Plural |
|---|---|
| everyone | all |
| everybody | |
| everything | |
| either | |
| each | |

The pronoun *all* is singular if it refers to things that cannot be counted as individual items (*all the money, all the air, all the mustard*). It is plural if it refers to things that can be counted as individual items (*all the dimes, all the books, all the cats*).

The following sentences show how some of these indefinite pronouns can be used. The pronouns that serve as subjects of the sentences are printed in boldface, and the verbs are printed in italics.

**3**

**Everyone** *is* here.

**Everybody** *knows* the answer to that question.

**Either** of these books *is* very good.

**Each** of my friends *is* in my school.

**All** the students *are* going to the game tomorrow.

**All** the money *is* gone.

■ **3 n   Pronouns That Refer to *some***

These indefinite pronouns refer to *some* people or things. They do not refer to any particular one of a group.

| Singular | Plural | Singular or Plural |
|----------|--------|--------------------|
| someone | both | some |
| somewhere | few | enough |
| somebody | many | more |
| something | several | most |

Here are sentences that use some of these pronouns. Again, notice whether the verbs are singular or plural.

**Someone** *is* knocking at the door.

**Something** *is* wrong with this clock.

**Both** of these students *are* good in math.

**Many** of the questions *were* very difficult.

**Some** of the people *are* still in the meeting.

**Some** of the money *is* still here.

**Most** of the students *were* on the playground.

**Most** of the jelly *was* all over the floor.

How can you decide which verb to use with the pronouns that can be *either* singular *or* plural?  Often you can look at the noun that comes after pronouns such as *some* or *more* or *most* and see what kind of noun it is.

> If the noun can be used to name a number of *individual* people or places or things, then the pronoun that comes before it is plural and requires a plural verb.

**Some** of the students *are* waiting at the door.
(Each *student* is an individual. *Students* is plural.)

**Most** of the people *enjoy* good weather.
(Each *person* is an individual. *People* is plural.)

**Some** of the dogs *are* running in the park.
(Each *dog* is an individual animal. *Dogs* is plural.)

> If the noun is a very *general* one and cannot be used to name individual people or objects, then the pronoun that comes before it is singular and requires a singular verb.  Some nouns of this type are *food*, *money*, *water*, *air*, and *jelly*.  You cannot have one *air* or two *airs*, so these nouns are considered to be singular because they name one *category* of things that cannot be broken down into individual units.

**Some** of the water *is* leaking through the roof.

**Most** of the money *is* still in the bank.

**Some** of the food *is* in the refrigerator.

■ **3 o    Pronouns That Refer to *any***

Another group of indefinite pronouns refers to *any* person or place or thing. Most of these pronouns are singular, but one of them may be either singular or plural.

| Singular | Singular or Plural |
|---|---|
| anyone | any |
| anything | |
| anybody | |
| anywhere | |

These sentences show how some of these pronouns are used:

**Anyone** *is* welcome to come to the party.

**Anything** *is* possible if you work hard enough.

**Anybody** *is* welcome to visit the museum.

**Any** of the students *are* invited to help out.

**Any** of these books *is* sure to be helpful.

The meaning of *any* is determined by the person who is speaking or writing. If you want *any* to include *all* the people or things you are talking about, then the verb should be plural. This is the case in the sentence "Any of the students are invited to help out." If you want *any* to refer to any *one* of several things, then the verb is singular. You saw this in the sentence "Any of these books is sure to be helpful."

■ **3 p     Pronouns That Refer to *none***

One last group of indefinite pronouns is used to express a **negative** statement. These pronouns always suggest that *no* particular people or things are specified.

| **Singular** | **Singular or Plural** |
| --- | --- |
| nobody | none |
| nothing | |
| neither | |
| no one | |
| nowhere | |

The following sentences use some of these negative pronouns. You can use the singular pronouns correctly if you remember that *nothing* means "not *one* thing"; *no one* and *nobody* mean "not *one* single person." *Neither* means "not either *one*" and is always singular. The word *none* is usually singular and means "not *one*," but it can occasionally be used in the plural if the writer or speaker wants to refer to several people or things.

**Nobody** *knows* where they went.

**Nothing** *is* as bad as a toothache.

**No one** *left* before the game ended.

**Neither** of these books *is* very interesting.

Remember that *neither* is singular and is the subject of the sentence. It should be matched by the singular verb *is*. Don't be fooled just because the plural noun *books* comes just before the verb.

**None** of the football players *was* badly hurt.
(This stresses the idea that *not one* of the players
was hurt.)

**None** of the football players *were* badly hurt.
(This is another way of saying "No players were hurt.")

# Demonstrative Pronouns

Four pronouns can be used to point out something or to demonstrate what you are talking about. The word *demonstrate* means "to show or make clear." These demonstrative pronouns can be used alone and do not always require antecedents.

|  | **Singular** | **Plural** |
|---|---|---|
| To point out something close by: | this | these |
| To point out something far away: | that | those |

Here are some sentences using demonstrative pronouns:

**This** is the best one of all.

**These** will be just right.

**That** will never work!

**Those** are the books I wanted.

# *Check Your Understanding*

## Using Indefinite Pronouns
*Answers begin on p. 269.*

**1.** Here is a list of indefinite pronouns:

   most     somebody     anyone     all     everyone

Use one of these indefinite pronouns to take the place of the group of words printed in boldface in each sentence. Each pronoun should be used only once.

   1. **All the spectators** cheered when he hit a home run.
   2. Did **any person in this room** see what happened here?
   3. **A large part** of the wall collapsed.
   4. **Every single one** of the players on the team got a hit.
   5. **One of the people** in the room left the window open.

**2.** Here is another list of indefinite pronouns:

   neither     several     both     anyone     everyone

From this list, choose the pronoun that best fits the blank space in each sentence below. Each pronoun should be used only once. Be sure to check the *verb* in each sentence and make sure the pronoun agrees with it.

   1. Does _____ know where Tom is?

   2. I scraped _____ of my knees on the sidewalk.

   3. Be sure that _____ gets a copy of the instructions.

   4. _____ of the two bicycles was in good condition.

   5. _____ of the students brought pictures to school.

# *Check Your Understanding*

### Subject and Object Pronouns

**1.** These sentences all use *nouns* as subjects. Rewrite each sentence using a *personal pronoun* as the **subject** in place of the nouns. Here is an example:

> **John and Mark** are both on the team.
> **They** are both on the team.

1. **The king** rode by in his royal carriage.
2. **Anne** lived in a small town on the coast of Maine.
3. **All the fans** cheered when their team won the game.
4. **This book** needs to be repaired.
5. **My friends and I** hurried home after school.

**2.** These sentences use *nouns* as objects. Rewrite each sentence using a *personal pronoun* as the **object** in place of the noun. Here is an example:

> I left my books with **Tom**.
> I left my books with **him**.

1. We gave a party for **Lucy**.
2. I saw some of **my friends** downtown last Saturday.
3. Please put **this book** on the table over there.
4. I played baseball with **Ed** yesterday.
5. The teacher asked **Roy and me** to get some supplies.

# *Check Your Understanding*

## The Antecedent of the Pronoun

1. Draw an arrow from each pronoun back to the noun that is its **antecedent**. Here is an example:

Ellen said that **she** would be here in an hour.

1. Sometimes my dreams don't come true, but sometimes **they** do.

2. The team got better and better, and **it** won lots of games.

3. My dog is not very big, but **he** makes a lot of noise.

4. My friends and I went to a movie, and then **we** took the bus back home.

5. Cindy didn't know that **she** had won first prize in the contest.

## Using Pronouns with Nouns

1. Correct the pronouns that are used with nouns.

1. **Us students** were glad when vacation began.
2. The teacher let **we boys** go out at recess.
3. **Us swimmers** won a trophy last year.
4. They gave **we girls** a chance to play volleyball.

2. These sentences use pronouns in compound subjects and compound objects. Change the pronouns that are used incorrectly.

1. **Me** and Ed couldn't wait for the game to start.
2. They wanted to give Ellen and **I** a nice present.
3. **Him and me** were supposed to be next in line.
4. He said he tried to call Tom and **I** four times.
5. This package came for Sarah and **I**.

# Check Your Understanding

## Possessive Pronouns

1. Use the correct **possessive pronouns** in place of the pronouns given in parentheses.

    1. Please give Susan (she) books.
    2. I think this is (they) dog.
    3. Evan lost (he) watch somewhere on the playground.
    4. I saw (you) brother when I was at the store.
    5. One of the tractors lost (it) steering wheel.

2. Notice that the pronouns in parentheses are not correct. Change the words in parentheses so that they become **possessive pronouns** that can stand alone. Here is an example:

    This book is (me). This book is **mine**.

    1. That pencil must be (you).
    2. Are these coats (us)?
    3. I don't know which hat is (her).
    4. I believe this desk is (him).
    5. These chairs must be (them).

3. These possessive pronouns will be used in the following sentences:

    theirs        yours        mine        ours        hers

    Now notice the words printed in italics in the second sentence of each example below. When you write these pairs of sentences on your paper, use a single possessive pronoun from the list above to take the place of the words in italics. Here is an example:

    Our car is parked here. Where is *your car*?
    Our car is parked here. Where is **yours**?

    1. Her books are over there. I can't find *my books* anywhere.
    2. His shoes are soaked. Did *your shoes* get wet, too?
    3. Our leaves are all raked. Have they raked *their leaves* yet?
    4. John's cap is over there. Where is *her cap*?
    5. Their house has been painted. *Our house* will be painted tomorrow.

# *Check Your Understanding*

## Using *who, whom,* and *whose*

**1.** Use the pronoun **who**, **whom**, or **whose** that fits each blank space.

    1.  Find out _____ is at the door.

    2.  _____ bike is standing out in the rain?

    3.  _____ should I see when I get there?

    4.  I'm not sure _____ books these are.

    5.  _____ is waiting to see me?

    6.  By _____ was the speech given?

**2.** Each of these sentences begins with *who* and ends with a preposition. Rewrite the sentences so that the correct pronoun *whom* is used. Also change the order of words so that the prepositions *for, with, by, to,* and *from* come before the pronoun. Here is an example:

> **Who** were you talking to?
> **To whom** were you talking?

    1.  Who were they asking for?
    2.  Who are you going to the game with?
    3.  Who was the package delivered by?
    4.  Who was this letter addressed to?
    5.  Who did you get that idea from?

# Verbs

You know that the sentence contains a subject and a predicate. The *predicate* is the part of the sentence that tells what happens to the subject. The **verb** is the most important part of speech within the predicate.

> • **Verbs** tell what the subject of the sentence *is* or what it is *doing*. Verbs express an action or help to make a statement complete.

Some sentences contain a single verb in the predicate:

Fish *swim*.

The wind *blows*.

I *play* in the school band.

We *watched* a TV program last night.

Other sentences may contain two or more verbs in the predicate:

He *slipped* and *fell* on the icy sidewalk.

George *is reading* a book about spiders.

I *have seen* that movie three times.

They *will travel* to New Orleans at Christmas.

Ellen *may have gone* to the park after school.

In this chapter you will see many ways that verbs can be used and combined in sentences.

**4**

## ■ 4 a     Base Words and Inflections

As you saw in Section **2d**, a **base word** is a complete word that has its own meaning and can stand on its own. With verbs, the base form is usually the one used with the pronoun *I*: *I talk*; *I see*; *I run*; *I walk*; and so on. Verbs also involve the use of **inflections**, which are usually letters added to the end of a base word to show that the word is being used in a variety of ways. For example, the verb *look* is a base word, while *looks*, *looked*, and *look**ing*** are inflected forms of that verb. Some verbs require inflections that involve other changes in spelling, such as *am, are, is* for the verb *be*.

In the following sentences each of the verbs is a base word:

I **play** baseball every Saturday in the summer.

The dogs **run** and **chase** each other all the time.

Jet planes **fly** very fast and **use** lots of fuel.

## ■ 4 b     Action Verbs

We often associate verbs with physical actions. These verbs tell what the subject of the sentence does: *walk, run, jump, hit, throw, work, carry, lift, play,* and *travel*, for example.

Other verbs are associated with doing things that may not require great physical effort. Even so, these are still action verbs because they require us to *do* something: *think, see, hear, read, write, listen, watch, know, remember,* and *learn,* for example.

## ■ 4 c     Verbs with Direct Objects

You know that some complete sentences can contain *only* a subject and a verb.

Birds fly.

Fish swim.

Volcanoes erupt.

In these sentences the predicate is complete because each verb tells what the subject *itself* does. However, there are other verbs that must be followed by more information in order to make the predicate complete.

Look at the following groups of words. Do these contain enough information to qualify as complete sentences?

They *carried*.

Elmo *hit*.

We *saw*.

Each group of words does have a subject and a verb. In fact, each sentence ends with an *action verb*. However, after we read each group of words, we are left with these questions:

They *carried* **WHAT**?

Elmo *hit* **WHAT**?

We *saw* **WHAT** or **WHOM**?

Obviously it is not *always* enough to have only a subject and a verb. In each example you just saw, the predicate was incomplete. Each verb needs to be followed by words that tell **WHAT** or **WHOM** in order to complete the meaning of the sentence.

They carried the heavy **package** for me.

Elmo hit the **ball** over the fence.

We saw **them** yesterday.

Now we have made the predicate complete by providing words that tell *what* was carried or hit and *who* was seen. Each of these words is a noun or a pronoun, sometimes preceded by modifiers, and each of these nouns or pronouns is a **direct object**.

**4**

> • The **direct object** is a noun or pronoun in the predicate that receives the action of the verb. It completes the meaning of the sentence by answering the question **WHAT?** or **WHOM?** after an action verb.

Look at some more sentences that contain direct objects:

I wrote a long **letter** to her last week.

They found the missing **necklace** behind the couch.

In order to understand how these sentences are constructed, we can make a simple diagram that focuses on the words of greatest importance: the *subject*, the *verb*, and the word that *completes* the meaning of the sentence. In the examples you just saw, the *direct object* was the word that completed the sentence by receiving the action of the verb.

As we explained in Chapter 1, diagrams show the most important words of each sentence on a *base line*. A vertical line through the base line separates the subject from the verb. A shorter vertical line above the base line separates the verb from the direct object.

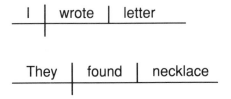

You will find out more about direct objects in Chapter 8. For now, remember that many action verbs are often followed by a direct object which completes the sentence by receiving the action of the verb.

## ■ 4 d    Verb Tenses

In the sentences you have seen so far, the action verbs told *what* was happening and *when* it was happening. In order to tell when something happens, each verb must be used in the correct *tense*. The **tense** of the verb is the particular form that tells you *when* an action takes place. We will look first at the three verb tenses that are used most often:

- **Present tense** tells about things that are happening when the sentence is being written or spoken. It is also used to tell about things that happen over and over again.
- **Past tense** tells about things that have already happened and are completed.
- **Future tense** tells about things that will happen tomorrow or next week or at some time to come.

# Regular Verbs

Many verbs follow a consistent pattern of inflections in the present, past, and future tenses. These are called **regular verbs**. In the next three sections you will see how these three tenses are formed with regular verbs.

In Section **3a** you saw an explanation of the terms **first person**, **second person**, and **third person**. Here is a review of those terms; notice how they apply to *verbs*.

- The **first person** is the person who is **speaking** (or writing).
- The **second person** is the person who is **spoken to.**
- The **third person** is the person or thing that is **spoken about.**

■ **4 e    Regular Verbs in the Present Tense**

- In the present tense, the base form is used most of the time. Only the third person singular requires an inflection.

Here you see how the regular verb *look* is written in the present tense with each of the personal pronouns:

**4**

|  | **Singular** | **Plural** |
|---|---|---|
| **First person** | I look | we look |
| **Second person** | you look | you look |
| **Third person** | he, she, it look**s** | they look |

The inflections for the *third person singular* are easy to remember.

> - Most verbs add *s* in the third person singular.
> - Some verbs add *es* in the third person singular. These are verbs that end with the following sounds and spellings:
>     /s/*s*, *ss*: miss, misses
>     /sh/*sh*: push, pushes
>     /ch/*ch*, *tch*: catch, catches
>     /ks/*x*: mix, mixes

The inflections *s* and *es* are very important. They are added to the verb after the pronouns *he*, *she*, *it*, and any *singular* noun that is the subject of the sentence.

Eddie *plays* on my soccer team.

My uncle Bob *fixes* my bike when it's broken.

Marie *helps* her brother with his homework every day.

The tree limb *touches* the window of my room.

Our puppy *chews* on everything in the house.

The statue *rests* on a large foundation.

The water *rushes* down the hill and *splashes* on the rocks.

### ■ 4 f    Regular Verbs in the Past Tense

When verbs are used to tell about things that have already happened, an inflection is added to show the **past tense**.

• Regular verbs always add the inflection **ed** to form the past tense. This inflection is used in all singular and plural forms.

|  | **Singular** | **Plural** |
|---|---|---|
| **First person** | I looked | we looked |
| **Second person** | you looked | you looked |
| **Third person** | he, she, it looked | they looked |

Use of the inflection **ed** in the past tense is the most important characteristic of regular verbs. It is the thing that establishes the *regular* pattern.

Later you will see some *irregular verbs* that do not add **ed** to form the past tense.

### ■ 4 g    Regular Verbs in the Future Tense

Verbs can be used to tell about something that may happen in the future.

• Add the word *will* before the base form of the verb in order to create the **future tense**.

This pattern is used in the singular and the plural.

|  | **Singular** | **Plural** |
|---|---|---|
| **First person** | I will look | we will look |
| **Second person** | you will look | you will look |
| **Third person** | he, she, it will look | they will look |

Here are a few sentences that use verbs in the future tense:

We *will see* them tomorrow afternoon.

They *will go* to Canada next summer.

I *will lock* the door when I leave.

You *will enjoy* that book when you read it.

In some situations, the word *shall* can be used to form the future tense. Usually this verb is used in the first person, singular or plural. *Shall* can be used in declarative sentences, although it is more likely to appear in formal writing than in informal conversation.

I *shall see* who is at the door.

We *shall arrive* before noon.

When *shall* is used in everyday speech, it usually appears as part of a question.

*Shall* I *answer* the phone for you?

*Shall* we *ask* someone for directions?

# Irregular Verbs

A number of important verbs do *not* add the inflection **ed** to form the past tense. These are called **irregular verbs**. Some irregular verbs also have unusual spellings even in the present tense. In this chapter we will look at two of the most important irregular verbs. In Chapter 8 you will find information on other irregular verbs.

## ■ 4 h    The Irregular Verb *be*

The most important irregular verb is *be*, as it is spelled in its base form. Here is the verb *be* in the present tense:

## PRESENT TENSE

|  | Singular | Plural |
|---|---|---|
| First person | I am | we are |
| Second person | you are | you are |
| Third person | he, she, it is | they are |

You can see how irregular this verb is. The base form *be* does not appear at all in the present tense, although you will see that it is used in some other situations. Also, there are three different forms of the verb: *am* for the first person singular, *is* for the third person singular, and *are* for all the others.

In the past tense, the verb *be* follows this pattern:

## PAST TENSE

|  | Singular | Plural |
|---|---|---|
| First person | I was | we were |
| Second person | you were | you were |
| Third person | he, she, it was | they were |

Here the same form (*was*) is used in the first and third person singular. *Were* is used with *you* and all the plural forms.

In the future tense, the base form *be* is combined with the verb *will*.

## FUTURE TENSE

|  | Singular | Plural |
|---|---|---|
| First person | I will be | we will be |
| Second person | you will be | you will be |
| Third person | he, she, it will be | they will be |

### ■ 4 i The Irregular Verb *have*

This verb is not quite as irregular as was the verb *be*. In the present tense, the verb *have* uses the base form except in the third person singular, where it is spelled *has*.

## PRESENT TENSE

|  | Singular | Plural |
|---|---|---|
| First person | I have | we have |
| Second person | you have | you have |
| Third person | he, she, it has | they have |

In the past tense, the spelling changes to *had* in singular and plural.

### PAST TENSE

|  | **Singular** | **Plural** |
|---|---|---|
| **First person** | I had | we had |
| **Second person** | you had | you had |
| **Third person** | he, she, it had | they had |

In the future tense, the verb *will* is combined with the base form of the verb *have*.

### FUTURE TENSE

|  | **Singular** | **Plural** |
|---|---|---|
| **First person** | I will have | we will have |
| **Second person** | you will have | you will have |
| **Third person** | he, she, it will have | they will have |

# Using Verbs in Combination

As you have seen, verbs can be used individually or they can be joined in various combinations.

■ **4 j     Main Verbs and Helping Verbs**

In earlier sections you saw that the verb *will* was combined with the base form of another verb to form the *future tense*.

I *will look* for your book tomorrow.

They *will arrive* next Tuesday.

We *will finish* the job as soon as possible.

In these examples, the words *look*, *arrive*, and *finish* are the **main verbs**. They are the verbs that tell what the subject is doing. The verb *will* in each sentence is called a **helping verb**. It tells that the action will take place in the future.

- The **main verb** tells exactly what the subject is or what it is doing. The main verb expresses the most important action in the sentence or gives us the most important information about the subject.
- The **helping verb** is used in combination with the main verb. It helps to mark the time of the action.

In addition to *will*, two of the most important helping verbs are *be* and *have*. Here are some sentences showing how the various forms of the verb *be* are used as helping verbs before main verbs:

I *am going* to see him next week.

You *are looking* in the wrong place.

He *is coming* back this afternoon.

We *are working* on the back porch.

They *are running* in the next race.

I *was watching* for the bus to arrive.

They *were playing* baseball in the school yard.

The next sentences show *have* used as a helping verb.

I *have waited* two hours for him.

We *have walked* five miles today.

He *has looked* everywhere for his turtle.

In Chapter 8 of this book you will learn more about main verbs and helping verbs. For now, it is important to realize that verbs can be used in various combinations to tell *what* happened and to tell *when* it happened.

**4**

## ■ 4 k    Linking Verbs

You have seen verbs used to tell about things that happen in the present or that happened in the past or that will happen in the future. There is still another way to use verbs such as *be*, *seem*, *feel*, and *appear*. These words can be used to *link* the subject with other parts of the sentence.

> • A **linking verb** is used to connect the subject of a sentence with other words in the predicate. The words in the predicate are usually nouns or adjectives. Linking verbs do not express action, but they do tell what the subject *is* or what it is *like*.

Look at these three pairs of sentences using the verb *be*. Notice the words that are printed in boldface in each sentence.

**John** is *my friend*. *My friend* is **John**.

**Mrs. Jones** is *my teacher*. *My teacher* is **Mrs. Jones**.

**The Greens** are *our neighbors*. *Our neighbors* are **the Greens**.

Is there any real difference between the first and second sentence in each pair? Doesn't "John is my friend" mean the same as "My friend is John"?

Yes, the first sentence in each pair says basically the same thing as the second sentence in the pair. The subject of each sentence is linked by the verb *is* or *are* to the words in the predicate.

In these sentences, the forms of the verb *be* were used as **linking verbs**. They did not tell us what someone *did*, but they did tell us who someone *is*. This is what linking verbs do: they *connect* the subject with additional information in the predicate.

Here are some more sentences using other verbs. Can you see that these sentences are similar to the three pairs of sentences you just saw?

This pizza *tastes* great!

He *feels* much better today.

Those people *seem* very friendly.

She *appears* very tired today.

These books *look* very interesting.

The audience *grew* quiet when the performance began.

The insulation will help the house *stay* warm.

Some clothes *become* unfashionable after a short time.

These sentences use verbs that connect each subject to more information in the predicate. Each sentence tells how someone *feels* or *seems* or how something *tastes* or *looks*. These are all linking verbs because they tell us something *about* the subject of each sentence; they do not tell us what the subject *did*.

Look back at the group of sentences you just saw. Try to substitute a form of the verb *be* in place of verbs such as *feel* or *seem* or *look*.

This pizza *is* great!

He *is* much better today.

Those people *are* very friendly.

She *is* very tired today.

And so on . . .

The meaning of each sentence does not change. This is how you can tell that words such as *taste* and *feel* and *seem* are used as linking verbs in these sentences.

Sometimes the same word can be an action verb *or* a linking verb, depending on how it is used. In the groups of sentences below, the verb in the first sentence of each pair tells what the subject *does*. In the second sentence of each pair, the same verb tells what the subject *is* or what it is *like*.

The ghost *appeared* out of nowhere.
They *appeared* tired after their long walk.

**4**

We *looked* all over the place for his dog.
The bear *looked* thin and scruffy.

In the dark we *felt* our way along the wall.
They *felt* cold when the wind started to blow.

Again, notice that it would be possible to use the verbs *were* or *was* in the second sentence of each pair without changing its meaning.

■ **41 Predicate Nouns and Pronouns**

Let's look again at the three pairs of sentences you saw near the beginning of Section **4k** on linking verbs.

**John** is my **friend**. My **friend** is **John**.

**Mrs. Jones** is my **teacher**. My **teacher** is **Mrs. Jones**.

The **Greens** are our **neighbors**. Our **neighbors** are the **Greens**.

All the boldfaced words are **nouns**, aren't they? Some are **proper nouns** (*John, Mrs. Jones, the Greens*) and others are **common nouns** (*friend, teacher, neighbor*).

In every sentence, the linking verb connects the *noun* in the subject to another *noun* in the predicate. The nouns that follow the verbs are called **predicate nouns**.

> • **Predicate nouns** follow linking verbs such as *be* or *seem*. Predicate nouns give more information about the subject.

In the sentences at the beginning of this section, you saw predicate nouns that gave us more information by telling us that someone is *my friend* or *my teacher* or *our neighbors*. Look at some more sentences that use predicate nouns to add information about the subject of each sentence. The predicate nouns are printed in boldface in the following examples:

Mr. Lopez is an **authority** on dinosaurs.

Cheetahs are spotted **cats** that live in Africa.

Mrs. Garcia is the **mayor** of our town.

Fred became the **captain** of the team.

Susan will be the **speaker** this afternoon.

Notice that linking verbs can be in the present, past, or future tense. The last two sentences show how the past tense (*became*) and the future tense (*will be*) are used.

Now we will look at the three most important words in each of these sentences: the *subject*, the *verb*, and the *predicate noun* that completes the meaning of the sentence. We can use a diagram similar to the one you saw in Section **4c** on direct objects. Here, however, a *slanted* line above the base line is used to separate the verb from the following predicate noun.

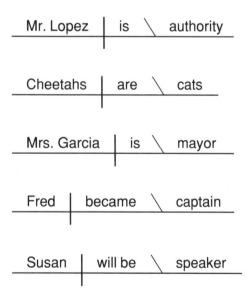

These simple diagrams help you see how the most important words in each sentence are related. In Chapter 9 you will see how other parts of the sentence can be diagrammed.

In the next examples, the subject is a pronoun (in italics). Each sentence also contains a predicate noun (in boldface).

**4**

*She* was the **winner** of the contest.

*He* is our team's biggest **fan**.

*I* was the **person** who answered the phone.

Now let's turn these sentences around. The subject is still in italics, but what has happened to the words in boldface?

The *winner* of the contest was **she**.

Our team's biggest *fan* is **he**.

The *person* who answered the phone was **I**.

Now the subjects are nouns, and the words in boldface have become **predicate pronouns**. If you compare the most important words in the two versions of each sentence, you can see why the *subject* form of the pronoun is still used when these words become predicate pronouns:

*She* was the **winner**.
The *winner* was **she**.

*He* is the **fan**.
The *fan* is **he**.

*I* was the **person**.
The *person* was **I**.

We can diagram the first pair of sentences to show why the subject pronoun is used in both situations.

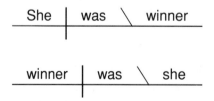

You probably won't use predicate pronouns very often; you are more likely to say "She was the winner" than to say "The winner was she." Even so, it is helpful to see how **linking verbs** allow you to write sentences which contain words in the predicate that tell what the subject *is*.

# Contractions

The following sentences were written by students your age. Pay particular attention to the words in boldface.

I **don't** feel very good.

He waited but they **didn't** come.

Are you sure **you'll** be all right?

She said, "**I've** got an idea!"

I **can't** answer that question.

**Who's** going to tell them what happened?

**I'm** a shoe. My name is Footy. **I'm** trapped in a pile of sneakers. **It's** very dark.

The words in boldface are called **contractions**.

> • A **contraction** joins two words in a shortened form. An **apostrophe** (') is used to take the place of letters that are left out of one of the words.

In the sentences you just saw, each contraction combines a verb with one other word.

## ■ 4 m    Verbs Followed by *not*

Every day you use contractions in which a verb is followed by the word *not*.

> • When *not* is used after a verb, the *o* can be omitted and replaced by an apostrophe. This forms the contraction *n't* that is joined with the verb.

Here are some examples of these contractions involving the irregular verbs *be* and *have* followed by *not:*

you are not - you aren't
she is not - she isn't
he was not - he wasn't
they were not - they weren't

I have not - I haven't
he has not - he hasn't
we had not - we hadn't

Look back at the various forms of *be* and *have* in Sections **4h** and **4i** to find other possible combinations that can be used with *not* to form contractions.

Notice that there is no contraction listed for *I am not*. This is because there is no way to combine *am* and *not* using an apostrophe. Instead, this contraction is formed by joining the pronoun and the verb: *I am not* becomes *I'm not*. In Section **4n** you will learn more about contractions that combine pronouns with verbs.

Here are some sentences that use these contractions:

You aren't going back in the haunted house, are you?

She isn't coming to school today.

He wasn't sure where he left his baseball bat.

They weren't able to see him when they were in town.

I haven't been able to find my bookbag.

He hasn't arrived yet.

We hadn't finished the lawn before the storm began.

Other verbs are often combined with *not* to form contractions. Here are some that are used most frequently:

you do not - you don't
it does not - it doesn't
they did not - they didn't

I can not - I can't
they could not - they couldn't
we should not - we shouldn't
you would not - you wouldn't

I could not - I couldn't
you would not - you wouldn't
they should not - they shouldn't

When *not* is combined with the verb *will* to form a contraction, it changes to *won't*.

I will not - I won't        we will not - we won't
he will not - he won't      they will not - they won't

There is a practical reason for this change. It would be almost impossible to pronounce *willn't* if we tried to use this as a contraction for *will not*. The sound of the vowel has been changed to make it blend with the shortened form of the word *not*.

Remember that the contraction **n't** shows that the letter **o** has been omitted from the word *not*. Don't make the mistake of writing *do'nt* or *is'nt* or *ca'nt*.

## ■ 4 n    Pronouns Combined with Verbs

Another kind of contraction can be formed by joining a pronoun with a verb. In these contractions, the spelling of the pronoun is not changed. Instead, the first letter or two of the verb is omitted and replaced by an apostrophe. For example, *I am* becomes *I'm*, and *we have* becomes *we've*.

### •  Pronouns Combined with *be*

Many contractions combine pronouns with the verb *be* in its various forms. Here are contractions involving the verb *be* in the present tense. The apostrophe takes the place of the first letter in each verb: *am*, *are*, and *is*.

PRESENT TENSE

|  | Singular | Plural |
| --- | --- | --- |
| **First person** | I am - I'm | we are - we're |
| **Second person** | you are - you're | you are - you're |
| **Third person** | he is - he's | they are - they're |
|  | she is - she's |  |
|  | it is - it's |  |

**I'm** sure you will like that movie.

**We're** leaving as soon as the rain stops.

I hope **you're** going to meet us there.

**He's** one of my best friends.

**She's** on the school basketball team.

**It's** snowing harder now.

Remember that the contraction *it's* uses an apostrophe to show that it is a shortened form of the words *it is*. Do not confuse this with the possessive pronoun *its*, which is not a contraction and does not contain an apostrophe.

**It's** very cold today. (**It is** very cold today.)

The tree has lost all **its** leaves. (The tree has lost all the leaves that **belonged to it**.

You will often find a contraction involving the pronoun *who* followed by the verb *is*:

**Who's** going with me to the game?

I don't know **who's** planning to pick us up.

Contractions are not usually used in the past tense of the verb *be*. There is no contraction for the first person *I was*. Contractions for the third person would look exactly like the present tense (*he's, she's, it's*). Contractions involving *were* with plural pronouns would also look exactly like the contractions in the present tense (*we're, you're, they're*).

The future tense of *be* will be considered when we look at contractions involving the verb *will* later in this section.

• **Pronouns Combined with *have***

Here are contractions combining pronouns with the verb *have* in the present tense. The apostrophe replaces the first *two* letters in the verbs *have* and *has*.

|  | Singular | Plural |
|---|---|---|
| **First person** | I have - I've | we have - we've |
| **Second person** | you have - you've | you have - you've |
| **Third person** | he has - he's | they have - they've |
|  | she has - she's |  |
|  | it has - it's |  |

In the past tense, the apostrophe replaces the first *two* letters in the verb *had*.

|  | Singular | Plural |
|---|---|---|
| **First person** | I had - I'd | we had - we'd |
| **Second person** | you had - you'd | you had - you'd |
| **Third person** | he had - he'd | they had - they'd |
|  | she had - she'd |  |
|  | it had - it'd |  |

The next group of sentences uses contractions involving the verbs *have* and *had*.

I've (I have) been looking for you everywhere.
She's (She has) gone to get some more mustard.
We've (We have) been waiting all day for this TV show.

You'd (You had) better not eat too much pizza.
We'd (We had) been waiting for him for an hour.
They'd (They had) watched cartoons for two hours.

## • Pronouns Combined with *will* and *would*

When the verb *will* is combined with a pronoun to form a contraction, the apostrophe takes the place of the first two letters in the verb.

|  | Singular | Plural |
|---|---|---|
| **First person** | I will - I'll | we will - we'll |
| **Second person** | you will - you'll | you will - you'll |
| **Third person** | he will - he'll | they will - they'll |
|  | she will - she'll |  |
|  | it will - it'll |  |

**4**

You can see how important it is to use the apostrophe in these contractions. In particular, the contractions *we'll* and *she'll* will look like the words *well* and *shell* if the apostrophe is omitted.

To form the **future tense** using contractions, simply use the contracted forms of the verb *will* and follow each one with the base form of the main verb. Here are sentences that use contractions in the future tense:

I'll be back in an hour.

You'll recognize him when you see him.

He'll call when he gets there.

She'll let us know what happens.

We'll leave on our trip in the morning

They'll finish repairing the roof tomorrow.

The verb *would* is the past tense of *will*, and it can also be used in contractions. This contraction is unusual because the apostrophe takes the place of all except the last letter in the word *would*.

**I'd** (I would) like to meet them.

**You'd** (You would) enjoy that movie a lot.

**They'd** (They would) like to leave before noon.

You can see that this contraction (*'d*) is the same as the one for *had*. The context of the sentence lets you know which verb is being used.

Although *could* and *should* have spelling patterns similar to *would*, they are not used in contractions.

■ **4 o** **Nouns Combined with Verbs**

You have seen contractions used in the *third person* after the pronouns *he, she,* or *it.* These same contractions can be used after *nouns* as well.

You can use the **'s** contraction to represent *is* after a noun that names a person, place, or thing.

**John's** not here yet. (**John is** not here yet.)

**New York's** a great place to visit. (**New York is** a great place to visit.)

This **chair's** old and rickety. (This **chair is** old and rickety.)

The **'s** contraction representing *has* can also be used after nouns. Because **'s** can represent either *is* or *has*, you must look at the whole sentence to see which is intended. When **'s** is used to represent *has*, then *has* is usually a helping verb followed by another word which is the main verb. (You may want to review the information on *Main Verbs* and *Helping Verbs* in Section **4j**.)

**Ellen's** called home three times already. (**Ellen has** called home three times already.)

My **dog's** chewed up another shoe. (My **dog has** chewed up another shoe.)

They **city's** bought two new fire trucks. (The **city has** bought two new fire trucks.)

Notice that words such as *Ellen's* and *dog's* and *city's* could be possessive nouns if they were followed by another noun. By looking at the whole sentence, you can tell that **'s** a contraction of the verbs *is* or *has*, especially if these words are followed by another verb.

The **'ll** contraction can be used after nouns, but this does not happen often. It can be used to represent a kind of slurred pronunciation that imitates the way we might sometimes speak.

**Mike'll** call you when he gets back. (**Mike will** call you when he gets back.)

Our **car'll** go faster than yours. (Our **car will** go faster than yours.)

# Agreement between Subject and Verb

When you write sentences, one of the most important things to watch for is the agreement between the **subject** and the **verb**. When the subject is a *singular* noun or pronoun, it is matched with a *singular* verb. When the subject is a *plural* noun or pronoun, it is matched with a *plural* verb.

## ■ 4 p   Agreement between Nouns and Verbs

When the subject and the verb are close together in the sentence, it is usually not difficult to make sure that they agree. In the next sentences the nouns in the subject are printed in boldface. The verb is printed in italics.

**Joan** *likes* books about space travel.

**Bill and Ellen** *wait* for the school bus.

Sometimes there may be several other words between the subject and the verb. When this happens, check carefully to be sure that the subject and the verb agree. In the next sentences the nouns in the subject are again printed in **boldface** and the verb is printed in *italics*.

**A dog** that can do tricks *is* fun to own.

**The people** across the street *are* our friends.

In the first sentence, the words *tricks is* may look wrong at first, but you must realize that *tricks* is not the subject. The verb *is* agrees with the singular subject, *dog*. In the second sentence, the words *street are* might also look wrong if you thought that *street* was the subject. Here, the plural verb *(are)* agrees with the plural subject *(people)*.

The following illustrations show how the subject and the verb agree in each of these sentences. The words that come between the subject and the verb are moved to a position below the subject.

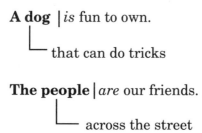

**A dog** | *is* fun to own.
 └── that can do tricks

**The people** | *are* our friends.
 └── across the street

■ **4 q    Agreement between Pronouns and Verbs**

We have always looked at verbs in the first person, the second person, and the third person to see how they should be used with **personal pronouns**.

> **I write** notes.

> **You write** letters.

> **She writes** books.

The most important personal pronouns to watch for are those in the **third person singular**: *he*, *she*, and *it*. In the present tense, the verb usually requires the inflection *s* or *es* in order to agree with these pronouns. This is also true when any singular noun (common or proper) is the subject.

> He *runs* around the track every day.

> She *runs* to catch up with her friends.

> A small stream *runs* past my house.

> It *runs* over its banks whenever it rains.

> The Mississippi River *runs* into the Gulf of Mexico.

• **Indefinite Pronouns and Demonstrative Pronouns**

You saw in Chapter 3 that there are also **indefinite pronouns** and **demonstrative pronouns** in addition to personal pronouns. Some of these indefinite and demonstrative pronouns are clearly singular and should be used with a singular verb: *everybody*, *each*, *someone*, *anybody*, *no one*, *this*, and *that*, for example.

> Everybody is back on the bus.

> Someone has the book I need.

> No one knows what happened.

> This is a great glass of lemonade!

Other indefinite and demonstrative pronouns are plural and should be used with a plural verb. The plural pronouns are *both*, *few*, *many*, *several*, *these*, and *those*.

Both of the books are worth reading.

Many saw the latest eclipse of the moon.

Several of the speakers were interesting.

These are the worst pickles I ever ate!

A few indefinite pronouns can be singular or plural, depending on the other words that were used with them. These pronouns are *all*, *some*, *more*, *most*, *any*, and *none*.

All of the air *has* leaked from the tire.

All of the cookies *are* broken.

> When a pronoun is used as the subject of a sentence, it must be followed by a verb that agrees with it. Singular subjects require singular verbs, and plural subjects require plural verbs.

Also remember that the verb must agree with the subject pronoun even if several other words come between the subject and the verb.

**Each** of these books *is* very interesting.

**Some** of the students *are* still outside.

In the first sentence, the pronoun *each* is singular and is matched with the verb *is*. In the second sentence, the plural pronoun *some* requires the verb *are*.

The next illustrations show you how the subject and verb agree. The words that come between each subject and verb are moved to a position below the subject.

**Each** │ *is* very interesting.
└── of these books

**Some** │ *are* still outside.
└── of the students

A few of the indefinite pronouns can be confusing. Be especially careful with these *singular* pronouns:

> **Each** of the hamsters *is* in its cage.
>
> **Either** of these bikes *is* worth repairing.
>
> **Neither** of the students *is* in class today.

When you use these pronouns, remember that you are actually saying *each one*, *either one*, and *neither one*. This will remind you to use a singular verb after these pronouns.

When indefinite pronouns are used with nouns that name individual people or objects, a singular verb is required. If nouns name people or objects that *cannot* be counted as individual units, a plural verb is required. Here are a few examples to remind you how indefinite pronouns can be used with singular and plural verbs:

> **All** of the books *are* on the table.
> **All** of the mayonnaise *is* on the floor.
>
> **Some** of my friends *live* close to me.
> **Some** of the money *is* still under the cushion.
>
> **Most** of the players *are* on the field.
> **Most** of the water *is* still in the basement.

You can count individual books or friends or players. This means that plural verbs are used when you talk about "all the books" or "some friends." However, you cannot count an individual mayonnaise ("one mayonnaise," "two mayonnaises") or an individual money or an individual water (although you can count *pieces* of money such as *dimes* or *quarters*, and you can count *glasses* or *gallons* of water). For this reason, words such as *all* and *some* are always used with singular nouns when they refer to categories of things such as water or money.

**4**

# *Check Your Understanding*

## The Verb Tenses
*Answers begin on p. 274.*

**1.** In each of these sentences a verb is given in its base form in parentheses. Use the verb in the **present tense** in each sentence.

1. He (be) one of my best friends.
2. My cat (chase) his tail all day.
3. She (have) a notebook just like mine.
4. His mom (encourage) him in everything he does.
5. This port (receive) many ships every day.

**2.** These sentences also give verbs in the base form (shown in parentheses). Use each verb in the **past tense**.

1. Last summer we (travel) to Idaho and Montana.
2. Yesterday I (be) caught in a big storm.
3. Last week we (visit) my grandparents.
4. Last month we (have) a good time at the beach.
5. I (stumble) in the dark and (bruise) my toe last night.

**3.** These sentences all show the base form of verbs in parentheses. Use each verb in the **future tense**.

1. Tomorrow I (go) to the dentist.
2. Next week we (exhibit) our pictures in the gallery.
3. They (launch) the weather balloon next Tuesday.
4. My uncle (arrive) some time next week.
5. I hope the teacher (explain) how to solve this problem.

**4**

# *Check Your Understanding*

### Action Verbs and Direct Objects; Main Verbs

1. Each of these sentences contains an **action verb** and a **direct object**. Underline the action verb once and the direct object twice. Then make a diagram that shows the subject, the verb, and the direct object. Here is an example:

   We <u>moved</u> the <u>logs</u> into the shed.   We | moved | logs

   1. The postman delivered a package to us yesterday.

   2. Leon dropped his watch into the mud.

   3. The flood covered many roads in the county.

   4. Yesterday we watched a movie about snakes and lizards.

   5. Divers located the ship under eighty feet of water.

2. Each of these sentences contains a **helping verb** followed by a **main verb**. Underline the helping verb *once*. Underline the main verb *twice*. Here is an example:

   I <u>have</u> <u>seen</u> that movie three times.

   1. I am going to Denver next summer.

   2. He had mowed the whole lawn before the rain started.

   3. This winter has been unusually cold and wet.

   4. We are planning a trip to Washington and New York.

   5. She is working on a science project.

   6. We have waited a long time for this game.

**4**

# *Check Your Understanding*

## Helping Verbs; Linking Verbs

1.  These sentences all contain **linking verbs**. First, underline the linking verb once. Then rewrite the sentence using a *different* linking verb. Sometimes you can use a form of the verb *be*, but other sentences may suggest different linking verbs such as *seem, feel, appear*, and so on. Here is an example:

    They <u>seemed</u> very tired.

    They **appeared** very tired. (They **were** very tired.)

    1.  The water was very cold.
    2.  That book seems interesting and amusing.
    3.  Our new neighbors are very friendly.
    4.  The dog looked wet and shaggy after the rain.
    5.  They were very nervous as the storm approached.

2.  Each of these sentences contains a **linking verb** and a **predicate noun**. Underline the linking verb once and the predicate noun twice. Then make a diagram that shows the subject, the verb, and the predicate noun. Here is an example:

    My dog <u>is</u> a <u>collie</u>.     dog | is \ collie

    1.  Maria's dad is a jet pilot.
    2.  Thomas Jefferson was the third president of the United States.
    3.  My math teacher is also a baseball coach in the summer.
    4.  Ms. Roberts became our new mayor last month.
    5.  Ellen was the winner of the first prize.
    6.  I am the captain of our team.

# *Check Your Understanding*

**Contractions; Agreement between Subject and Verb**

1. These sentences all contain a verb followed by the word *not*. Use a contraction that combines the verb with the word *not*. Here is an example:

> He **has not** come back yet.
> He **hasn't** come back yet.

   1. I **do not** know where he went.
   2. They **are not** at home and I can not locate them.
   3. I **have not** seen him all day.
   4. Ellen and Maria **were not** in school yesterday.
   5. The workers **had not** finished the job before the rain began.

2. These sentences contain a pronoun followed by a verb. Use a contraction that combines the pronoun with the verb. Here is an example:

> **She has** worked in the yard all afternoon.
> **She's** worked in the yard all afternoon.

   1. **I am** sure he will be back soon.
   2. **We are** going to the mountains next summer.
   3. **They have** been looking for their dog all day.
   4. **He is** one of my best friends.
   5. **She had** been traveling for three days.

3. In these sentences the subject and verb do not agree. Find the subject in each sentence and decide if it is singular or plural. Then change the **verb** so that it agrees with the subject.

   1. The students in my class is going to take a trip.
   2. John and Frank was the best players on the team.
   3. He always have a lot of fun at his cousin's house
   4. The men standing on the corner was waiting for the bus.
   5. The people who live next door has two dogs and a cat.

# 5

# Adjectives

Look at these sentences written by students your age. Notice the words printed in boldface.

The blast of **icy** wind came through the door.

A boy walked along a mountainside on a **warm** day in April.

He waited about **five** minutes and then went to his room.

She is a **serious** person, but she can also be **funny**.

Each of these boldfaced words tells more about another word in the sentence. Each of these words is an **adjective**.

> • **Adjectives** are words that modify nouns or pronouns.

When we *modify* something, we *change* it in some way. A noun or pronoun can be modified by other words which give the original word a more precise meaning. For example, the noun *wind* can be modified in a number of ways: a **cold** wind, a **hot** wind, a **strong** wind, a **light** wind, and so on. Each word in boldface is an adjective which makes the meaning of the noun *wind* more precise.

Adjectives often appear just before the nouns they modify, but sometimes an adjective may be separated from the word it modifies. You saw this in the sentence which ended "but she can also be **funny**." Here the adjective *funny* comes in the predicate, yet it still modifies the subject pronoun, *she*.

Throughout this chapter we will see adjectives used in a variety of ways.

**5**

## ■ 5 a    Articles

The adjectives *a*, *an*, and *the* are used very often. These three adjectives are called **articles**.

---

The articles *a* and *an* mean "one" or "any." They are used only in the *singular*.

- **A** is used before words beginning with a consonant.

- **An** is used before words beginning with a vowel.

  We had **a** test. It was **an** easy test.
  Garfield is **an** unusual cat. He is **a** very chubby cat.

---

The articles *a* and *an* simply indicate that we are talking about *one* person or thing. They do not specify exactly *which* one.

---

The article ***the*** can be used before *singular or plural* nouns. This word often refers to something that has already been specified.

  I have a new coat. This is **the** coat I just got.
  We found some old books. These are **the** books we found.

---

*The* is more definite than *a* or *an*. You can see the difference in these sentences.

  I was shopping for **a** scarf.

  I wanted **an** orange one with blue stripes.

  I found exactly **the** scarf I was looking for.

## ■ 5 b    Demonstrative Adjectives

There are four other adjectives that have a special name of their own. They modify words more precisely than articles do. These are the **demonstrative adjectives**:

| Singular | Plural |
|----------|--------|
| this | these |
| that | those |

> - **Demonstrative adjectives** indicate specific people or things. They tell us exactly *which* ones we are talking about.
> - The word *demonstrate* means "to show" or "to make clear."

*This* and *these* are used to specify people or things that are nearby or that have just been mentioned.

**This** book is very interesting.

**These** doughnuts are not very good.

*That* and *those* specify people or things that are at some distance or that were referred to earlier.

**That** tree is about to fall down.

**Those** people are waiting for the bus.

### ■ 5 c The Difference between Demonstrative Adjectives and Demonstrative Pronouns

In Chapter 3 we looked at **demonstrative pronouns**. Those pronouns are the same words that can be used as **demonstrative adjectives**. How can you tell the difference?

See if you can find a pattern in these pairs of sentences:

**This** biography of Lincoln is very good.
**This** is a very good biography of Lincoln.

**These** chairs are falling apart.
**These** are the chairs that are falling apart.

**That** movie was very exciting.
**That** was a very exciting movie.

**Those** shelves need to be painted.
**Those** are the shelves that need to be painted.

The first sentence of each pair begins with a demonstrative adjective. The second sentence in each pair begins with a demonstrative pronoun. Here is how to tell them apart:

---

**Demonstrative adjectives** are usually followed by the *nouns* they modify.

**That** *movie* was very exciting.

**Demonstrative pronouns** take the place of nouns. These pronouns are usually followed immediately by *verbs*.

**That** *was* a very exciting movie.

---

■  **5 d    Predicate Adjectives**

We have seen that adjectives can be used directly before the nouns they modify: an *icy* wind; a *warm* day; a *serious* person; and so on. Now we will look at another way of using adjectives.

Notice how the adjectives (written in boldface) are used in these sentences:

Bill and Tony were **alone** in the haunted house.

They had never felt so **afraid**.

The adjectives *alone* and *afraid* are used in the predicate of each sentence. In the first sentence, the adjective *alone* refers to the subject *Bill and Tony*. In the second sentence, the adjective *afraid* refers to the subject *They*. In these sentences, the words *alone* and *afraid* are **predicate adjectives**.

> • A **predicate adjective** follows a linking verb such as *be* or *feel* or *seem*. A predicate adjective is separated from the word it modifies.

Most adjectives that begin with *a-* can be used only as predicate adjectives. In the following examples you can see that these adjectives will not work if they are used directly before the words they modify. The second sentence in each pair shows how these *a-* adjectives should be used after linking verbs.

He was an **alone** boy. The boy was **alone.**

She was an **afraid** person. She was **afraid.**

We have seen that adjectives can modify both nouns and pronouns. In fact, we generally *must* use a predicate adjective if we want to modify a pronoun. Look at this pair of sentences:

That movie was **great**. It was very **exciting.**

In the first sentence, the predicate adjective *great* modifies the noun *movie*, which is the subject. In the second sentence, the predicate adjective *exciting* modifies the pronoun *it*, which is also the subject of the sentence. In each sentence, the subject and the predicate adjective are connected by the linking verb *was*.

Here are some more pairs of sentences that follow the pattern we have just seen:

The cookies tasted **good**. They were truly **delicious.**

Joan was very **happy**. She felt **pleased** after the visit.

Tom seemed **sad**. He appeared **unhappy** when they left.

Look at some more sentences that contain predicate adjectives (written in boldface):

Our neighbor's dog is very **large**.

This old oak tree is truly **enormous**.

The barn was soon **ablaze** after the lightning struck.

We can focus on the most important words in these sentences by using simple diagrams similar to the ones you saw in Section **41** on *predicate nouns*. In the following diagrams, each predicate adjective is written on the base line and is separated from the linking verb by a *slanted line*, just as predicate nouns were. Each predicate adjective modifies the subject of the sentence.

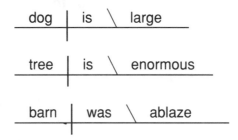

Predicate adjectives help you emphasize your description of a person or a thing. Look at the difference between sentences that place adjectives just *before* the nouns they define and sentences that place these adjectives *after* the nouns.

I have a very **large** dog.
My dog is very **large**.

This is a truly **enormous** tree.
This tree is truly **enormous**.

These are unbelievably **tiny** minnows.
These minnows are unbelievably **tiny**.

You can choose the type of sentence that best expresses the idea you want to convey to the reader.

## ■ 5 e    Adjectives That Tell *What Kind*

Many adjectives tell us something definite about the words they modify. In the following examples, the first sentence in each group simply makes a statement. The second and third sentences contain adjectives that tell us about the *size* or the *speed* of something.

> He caught a fish.
> It was a very **large** fish.
> The fish was very **large**.
>
> They have a dog.
> It is a **small** dog.
> Their dog is **small**.
>
> I saw a car at the race track.
> It was a very **fast** car.
> The car was very **fast**.
>
> We rode the elevator.
> It was a very **slow** elevator.
> The elevator was very **slow**.

The second sentence in each group uses an adjective *before* each noun. The third sentence uses a *predicate adjective* to give the same information found in the second sentence.

These adjectives tell *what kind* of thing we are reading or talking about. Other adjectives can describe the color, the shape, or the texture of something. When we want to describe what kind of think we are talking about, we often tell how it *looks*, *sounds*, *feels*, *smells*, or *tastes*.

> I like the **green** dress better than the **blue** one.
>
> She had a **colorful** poster on her wall.
>
> The **curved** stairway was made of iron.
>
> Did the **brilliant** light startle you?
>
> That was a **delicious** meal.
>
> Did you feel the **rough** surface of that wall?
>
> A **pleasant** aroma came from the kitchen.

**5**

## ■ 5 f  Adjectives That Tell *How Much* or *How Many*

Another important group of adjectives tells us what *quantity* of things we are talking about.

How could you eat only **one** cookie?

We have **two** dogs and **three** cats.

There are **twenty-three** students in my class.

All these number words tell us exactly how many things we are talking about. There is one important thing to keep in mind when numerals are used as adjectives:

> Whenever you spell out the numerals from **twenty-one** through **ninety-nine**, use a *hyphen* (-) to separate the two words.

I counted **thirty-three** cars and **twenty-nine** trucks.

There are **forty-seven** kinds of fish at the pet store.

There are other adjectives that give only a *general* idea of "how much" or "how many." These adjectives can indicate a small or a large number of people or things, but they do not give exact quantities.

We should wait a **few** minutes before we leave.

There are **several** books to choose from.

They saw **many** animals at the zoo.

We put **some** flowers in the vase.

We couldn't find **any** dishes that weren't broken.

When adjectives tell *how much* or *how many*, they are usually placed directly before the word they modify.

## ■ 5 g   Recognizing Adjectives: Using Suffixes

Many adjectives end with **suffixes** which tell us that the words are indeed adjectives.

> • A **suffix** is a syllable or syllables added to the *end* of a base word. Suffixes can create a new word, change the meaning of the base word, or allow a word to serve different functions within the sentence.

The suffix *-ous* almost always identifies a word as an adjective. Sometimes this suffix is added to nouns to change them to adjectives. The following examples use nouns in the first sentence of each pair and adjectives in the second:

> The actor's **fame** was well established. He was **famous** throughout the world.

> She showed great **courage**. She was very **courageous**.

> The storm placed the little ship in great **peril**. It made the voyage extremely **perilous**.

Here are some more adjectives that end with the suffix *-ous*. Some of these base words are also nouns (*nerve, joy, ridicule*).

| | | |
|---|---|---|
| nervous | ridiculous | enormous |
| joyous | anonymous | ominous |
| porous | contagious | tremendous |

The suffix *-y* is also often used to create adjectives. This suffix is sometimes added to nouns such as *fun* or *luck*.

| | | | |
|---|---|---|---|
| funny | merry | scruffy | silly |
| lucky | jolly | foggy | jumpy |
| happy | greedy | itchy | fiery |

When the *-y* suffix is added to the noun *fire*, notice that the spelling changes to *fiery*.

The following list shows other suffixes that may be used to create adjectives:

| Suffix | Adjectives |
|--------|------------|
| *-ful* | wonderful, hopeful, beautiful, useful |
| *-less* | hopeless, worthless, useless, endless |
| *-ish* | foolish, childish, squeamish, sluggish |
| *-ic* | basic, hectic, terrific, heroic |
| *-ive* | expensive, active, decisive, selective |
| *-able* | probable, usable, portable, enjoyable |
| *-ible* | terrible, horrible, visible, sensible |

Some of these suffixes can be used with other words and do not *always* indicate adjectives. In order to be sure that a word is an adjective, see if it can follow the word *very* to fit the blank space in this sentence.

This is a very _____ NOUN.

The last word can be any noun that makes sense with the word which precedes it.

This is a very **enjoyable** BOOK.

This is a very **sensible** DECISION.

This is a very **expensive** COAT.

This is a very **foolish** MISTAKE.

This is a very **useful** TOOL.

This is a very **ominous** SIGN.

Because the word *very* so often precedes adjectives, you can usually use this sentence pattern to find out whether or not a word is an adjective. However, it does not always apply to the small number of words such as *ablaze* and *aflame* that are used as predicate adjectives and are not followed by nouns.

# Using Adjectives to Make Comparisons

We have seen that adjectives can be used to *modify* nouns or pronouns by telling more about them. Adjectives can also be used to *compare* two or more things.

> Bill is fairly **tall**, but John is **taller** than Bill.
> Carlos is the **tallest** of all.

The word *tall* is an adjective in its base form. This is also called its **positive form**. In order to make comparisons we add *inflections* or make other changes in the positive form.

## ■ 5 h Adjectives That Add *er* and *est*

When comparisons are made, most adjectives add the following endings to the positive form.

> - Add the inflection *er* to compare two things. This is called the **comparative form** of the adjective.
> - Add the inflection *est* to compare more than two things. This is called the **superlative form** of the adjective.

Here you see the three forms of some familiar adjectives:

| Positive | Comparative | Superlative |
|----------|-------------|-------------|
| small | smaller | smallest |
| thick | thicker | thickest |
| fast | faster | fastest |
| slow | slower | slowest |

Many adjectives can add *er* and *est* without any change in the base form. Some other adjectives require changes in spelling when these endings are added. On the following pages you will see guidelines that can help you decide how to add inflections to adjectives. All examples are listed in the positive, comparative, and superlative forms.

**5**

- When an adjective ends with a short vowel followed by a single consonant, this final consonant is doubled before *er* and *est* are added.

   big, bigger, biggest
   hot, hotter, hottest
   flat, flatter, flattest
   mad, madder, maddest
   thin, thinner, thinnest

- We have seen that many adjectives end with **-y**. This suffix is usually the last syllable in a word of two or more syllables. Before adding *er* or *est*, this *y* is changed to *i*.

   funny, funnier, funniest
   happy, happier, happiest
   heavy, heavier, heaviest
   lucky, luckier, luckiest
   hungry, hungrier, hungriest
   pretty, prettier, prettiest
   tiny, tinier, tiniest

- When an adjective ends with *e*, drop this letter before adding *er* and *est*.

   wide, wider, widest
   brave, braver, bravest
   close, closer, closest
   fine, finer, finest

- When an adjective contains a **vowel digraph**, there is no change in the spelling of the word when inflections are added. (A *digraph* is a group of two letters with a single sound, such as *ai* in *rain*.)

   loud, louder, loudest           plain, plainer, plainest
   weak, weaker, weakest           proud, prouder, proudest
   broad, broader, broadest        cool, cooler, coolest
   sweet, sweeter, sweetest        brief, briefer, briefest

- Some adjectives end with **consonant digraphs** which represent a single sound. Other adjectives end with two consonants that are blended together. If an adjective ends with two consonants, do not make any change in the spelling of the word when the inflections *er* and *est* are added.

| | |
|---|---|
| rich, richer, richest | fresh, fresher, freshest |
| long, longer, longest | smooth, smoother, smoothest |
| cold, colder, coldest | hard, harder, hardest |
| quick, quicker, quickest | rough, rougher, roughest |

You can use the following guideline to help you decide how to add *any* ending to words:

> If the base word contains any kind of digraph (vowel or consonant) in the final syllable, do not change the spelling of that word when you add endings.

## ■ 5 i   Making Comparisons with *more* and *most*

Many adjectives contain more than one syllable. Most of these do not add *er* in the comparative form and *est* in the superlative form. Instead, they are preceded by other words that show a change in the quality expressed in the adjective.

To show an **increase** in size, degree, or quantity, make the following changes:

> - Use the word *more* for the comparative form of adjectives containing more than one syllable (*more difficult*).
> - Use the word *most* for the superlative form of adjectives containing more than one syllable (*most difficult*).

That is a **beautiful** painting, but this one is even **more beautiful**.
I think the painting over there is the **most beautiful** of all.

Here are some more adjectives that are preceded by *more* and *most* to show the comparative and superlative forms:

| | |
|---|---|
| afraid | awkward |
| expensive | exciting |
| graceful | important |
| generous | practical |
| natural | delicious |

### ■ 5 j Making Comparisons with *less* and *least*

When we want to show a **decrease** in the quality expressed in the adjective, we use other words to create the comparative form and the superlative form.

> • Use the word *less* for the comparative form of adjectives containing more than one syllable (*less difficult*).
> • Use the word *least* for the superlative form of adjectives containing more than one syllable (*least difficult*).

This movie was *exciting*, but it was *less exciting* than the one we saw yesterday.
The movie we saw last week was the *least exciting* of all.

Most of the adjectives that use *more* and *most* can also use *less* and *least*.

> When adjectives use the inflections *er* and *est* to show comparison, they should not be combined with *more* and *most* or *less* and *least*. Only one form of comparison is needed.

WRONG:  This frog is **more bigger** than that one.
RIGHT:   This frog is **bigger** than that one.

WRONG:  He was **more afraider** than I was.
RIGHT:   He was **more afraid** than I was.

## ■ 5 k    Making Comparisons with Irregular Adjectives

The following adjectives have special comparative and superlative forms. They do not add *er* and *est*.

good, better, best
bad, worse, worst
far, farther, farthest
some, more, most
many, more, most
much, more, most
little, less, least

*More* and *most* can also be used to show a *greater degree* of something and the *greatest degree* of something. *Less* and *least* can be used to show a *smaller degree* of something and the *smallest degree* of something. You do not always have to specify exactly how many things you are comparing.

There is **more** shade over there under that big tree.
We had **less** snow last winter than the winter before.

This is the **most** rain I've ever seen.
That was the **least** difficult test we've had.

Be careful with *worse*, which compares only two things, and *worst*, which compares more than two.

This pizza is *worse* than that one, but the pizza we had yesterday was the *worst* I ever ate.

# Adjectives in a Series

A *series* is a group of related words used one after another. Usually a series of words contains words of the same part of speech. Sometimes you may want to use two or more adjectives in a series to modify a noun.

## ■ 5 l    Using Two Adjectives in a Series

When there are *only* two adjectives in a series, they can often be written this way:

**5**

There were **several good** shows on TV last night.

They live in the **big purple** house on the corner.

It is not necessary to separate the adjectives because they *work together* to modify the noun. The pairs of adjectives would not make sense if they were reversed. For this reason, they should not be separated by a comma.

Now look at some more sentences that use two adjectives before the noun. Notice the difference in the way these adjectives are written.

A **large, heavy** object blocked the road.

The **harsh, cold** wind blew across the plains.

Here a comma is used to separate the two adjectives because they are *equally important* and each of them modifies the noun in a different way. In the first sentence, the object in the road happened to be large *and* heavy. However, it wouldn't *necessarily* have to be both. An object made of plastic could be large but light in weight, and an object made of stone could be small but heavy. It is important for the two adjectives to be given equal importance, and this is done by separating them with a comma.

The same thing is true in the second sentence. The wind could be harsh without necessarily being cold (it could have been hot). It might have been cold without being particularly harsh (it could have been blowing very gently). Here again, we use a comma to show that each adjective modifies the noun in its own way, and each adjective is as important as the other.

If the order of the two adjectives could be reversed, or if the word *and* could be used between them, then they should be separated by a comma.

He can be a stubborn, exasperating child.

He can be an exasperating, stubborn child.

(He can be a stubborn and exasperating child.)

■ **5 m      Using Three or More Adjectives in a Series**

Whenever there are *more* than two adjectives in a series, it is necessary to use commas to separate them. If three or more adjectives all run together, they might become confusing to the reader. Look at this example:

It was a **cold dark windy** day.

Here the adjectives come before the noun. Because there are three of them, the reader can become lost in the sentence. These three adjectives should be separated by **commas**.

It was a **cold, dark, windy** day.

When more than two **predicate adjectives** are used, commas separate each pair of adjectives. Also, a word such as *and* or *or* must be used before the last adjective in the series.

The day was **cold, dark, and windy**.

Look at some more sentences that use three adjectives. Some sentences show adjectives used just before the noun they modify. Other sentences use predicate adjectives that are separated from the word they modify.

We took a **long, boring, exhausting** trip.
Our trip was **long, boring, and exhausting**.

It was a **funny, exciting, clever** movie.
The movie was **funny, exciting, and clever**.

Remember that adjectives can also modify pronouns. They will usually be predicate adjectives and will follow the rules given earlier.

The weather was terrible. It was **cold**, **windy**, and **damp**.

My dog is a great friend. He is **playful**, **loyal**, and **smart**.

Ed's coat is missing. It is **brown**, **tan**, or **gray**.

There are other ways to write sentences that contain three or more adjectives. In the next examples the adjectives come before the noun and are separated by commas, but a word such as *and* or *or* is added before the last adjective.

We took a **long, boring, and exhausting** trip.

It was a **funny, exciting, and clever** movie.

**5**

Finally, it is possible to separate all the adjectives with words such as *and* or *or*. No commas will be needed at all. This works especially well with *predicate adjectives*.

We took a **long and boring and exhausting** trip.
Our trip was **long and boring and exhausting**.

It was a **funny and exciting and clever movie**.
The movie was **funny and exciting and clever**.

It was not a **pleasant or relaxing or enjoyable vacation**.
Our vacation was not **pleasant or relaxing or enjoyable**.

You will rarely want to use more than three adjectives in a series, but the same procedure is followed in every situation.

People can be **nice or mean or hateful or lovely**.
People can be **nice, mean, hateful, or lovely**.

# Proper Adjectives

When we named specific people, places, or things, we used **proper nouns**. These nouns were always capitalized.

**Spain** and **Italy** are countries in Europe.

Many proper nouns can also be used as proper adjectives.

The **Spanish** and **Italian** languages are related.

> • **Proper adjectives** are derived from proper nouns. Proper adjectives are always capitalized.

Some proper nouns can be used as proper adjectives without any change. In the next sentences, the names of states and cities are used as proper adjectives. Notice that each state or city is followed by a noun.

The **California** condor is a large vulture.

They brought **Maine** lobsters, **Wisconsin** cheese, and **Georgia** peaches.

The **London** fog can be very dense.

Sometimes it is necessary to add a special ending to change a proper noun to a proper adjective. Some proper adjectives end with *-an* or *-ian*, and others end with *-ish* or *-ese*. Here are a few proper nouns followed by their spellings as proper adjectives:

| Proper Noun | Proper Adjective |
|---|---|
| America | American |
| Mexico | Mexican |
| Rome | Roman |
| Africa | African |
| Germany | German |
| Russia | Russian |
| Italy | Italian |
| Egypt | Egyptian |
| Brazil | Brazilian |
| Canada | Canadian |
| England | English |
| Britain | British |
| Denmark | Danish |
| Sweden | Swedish |
| China | Chinese |
| Japan | Japanese |
| Portugal | Portuguese |
| Vienna | Viennese |

Here are a few sentences using some of these proper adjectives:

The **American** flag has red and white stripes.

They have a **Japanese** car, some **Danish** furniture, a **Siamese** cat, and a **German** shepherd dog.

**Canadian** winters are very long and cold.

We had **Chinese** food at an **Italian** restaurant in Omaha.

**5**

# *Check Your Understanding*

## Using Adjectives
*Answers begin on p. 279.*

**1.** Choose the correct adjective from those given in parentheses.

1. We had (a, an, the) very good time.
2. This is (a, an, the) unexpected development.
3. Have you heard about (this, these) discovery?
4. We will use (that, those) chemical in the experiment
5. (This, These) keys have been missing for a week.

**2.** These sentences use adjectives directly before the nouns they modify. Rewrite each sentence so that the noun comes near the beginning and the adjective is moved to the end of the sentence to become a **predicate adjective**. Here is an example:

> This is a very **interesting** *book*.
> This *book* is very **interesting**.

1. Those are extremely old trees.
2. That was a very easy test.
3. These are expensive rings and bracelets.
4. This is a delicious piece of pie.
5. That was an unusually long trip.

Notice that each of the five sentences begins with a demonstrative pronoun. What happens to this word when you rewrite each sentence?

# *Check Your Understanding*

3. In the following sentences you will see a word in parentheses. Use the appropriate suffix to change this word to an adjective. Here is an example:

> The lightning and the wind made me (nerve).
> The lightning and the wind made me *nervous*.

1. That was a (luck) break for you.
2. He is one of the most (fame) performers on television.
3. These flowers are very (beauty).
4. We had a (wonder) time at the party.
5. This was one of the most (enjoy) movies I have seen.

4. These sentences contain predicate adjectives. Underline the predicate adjective. Then make a diagram that shows the **subject**, the **verb**, and the **predicate adjective**. Here is an example:

> Her brother is very <u>tall</u>.　　brother | is \ tall

1. The water became very hot in the sunlight.
2. They seemed happy after winning the game.
3. The sailors were fortunate to escape the storm.
4. We felt extremely tired after the long walk.
5. I was glad when the test was over.
6. The runners appeared exhausted after the race.

**5**

# *Check Your Understanding*

## Making Comparisons with Adjectives

1.  In each of these sentences an adjective is given in parentheses. Use the suffixes *er* or *est* to write the **comparative form** or the **superlative form** as required in each case.

    1.  This is the (large) dinosaur ever discovered.
    2.  We need a (big) hammer for these large nails.
    3.  Isn't this tree (tall) than that one?
    4.  I just saw the (ugly) alligator in the world!

2.  Adjectives are written in parentheses in these sentences. Add the word *more* or *most* to write the **comparative form** or the **superlative form** as required in each case.

    1.  This coat is (practical) than that one.
    2.  That was the (important) decision he ever made.
    3.  I was (afraid) than he was.
    4.  That was the (interesting) book I ever read.

3.  The irregular adjectives in these sentences are given in their base form in parentheses. Use the **comparative form** or the **superlative form** as required.

    1.  This movie was (bad) than the one we saw last week.
    2.  Who has the (good) team in the league?
    3.  He ate (some) cookies than I did.
    4.  He scored the (many) points of anybody on the team.

# *Check Your Understanding*

## Adjectives in a Series; Proper Adjectives

1. Use the necessary commas to make the series of adjectives clear to the reader. You may have to add words such as *and* or *or* in some cases.

    1. The small heavy statue was made of marble.
    2. The game was long slow dull tiresome.
    3. We had some red ripe delicious tomatoes.
    4. All the speakers were bright witty clever.
    5. The brief intense storm did a lot of damage.

2. Each of these sentences contains proper nouns in parentheses. Make the alterations needed to change these proper nouns to **proper adjectives**.

    1. The (Sweden) coastline has many small inlets called *fjords*.
    2. Many (Rome) fountains were built centuries ago.
    3. The (Russia) language is very different from the (England) language.
    4. The (Africa) continent is home to many different animals.
    5. A large (Mexico) hat is called a *sombrero*.

# 6

# Adverbs

In Chapter 5 you saw that adjectives modify nouns or pronouns. In this chapter we will look at another part of speech that can be used to modify words *other* than nouns and pronouns. These modifiers are called **adverbs**.

> • **Adverbs** are words that modify verbs, adjectives, or other adverbs.

## Using Adverbs to Modify Verbs

Look at the words printed in boldface in these sentences. Also notice the words to which the arrows point.

They ran **quickly** to get out of the rain.

We left **early** so we could avoid the crowd.

She waited **inside** for the storm to stop.

These boldfaced words are **adverbs**. They modify the **verb** in each sentence by telling us **how** something happened, **when** it happened, or **where** it happened. Later we will see how adverbs modify adjectives and other adverbs.

■ **6 a    Adverbs Formed from Adjectives: The Suffix -*ly***

Many adverbs end with the suffix -*ly*. Remember that a **suffix** is a syllable or syllables added to the *end* of a base word. Suffixes can create a new word, change the meaning of the base word, or allow a word to serve different functions.

Often the suffix *-ly* is added to an **adjective** to change it to an **adverb**. Remember that an adjective can modify *only* a noun or a pronoun; it cannot modify a verb. In order to create an adverb that modifies a verb, we can add the suffix *-ly* to many adjectives. You can see this in the following sentences.

> It was a **clear** day for taking pictures. We **clearly** saw the hilltop across the valley.

In the first sentence the adjective *clear* modifies the noun *day*. In the second sentence the word has changed to the adverb *clearly*, which modifies the verb *saw*.

Here you see some adjectives that can be changed to adverbs by adding the suffix *-ly:*

| Adjective | Adverb | Adjective | Adverb |
|-----------|--------|-----------|--------|
| quick | quickly | slow | slowly |
| bad | badly | quiet | quietly |
| warm | warmly | real | really |
| final | finally | complete | completely |
| nice | nicely | true | truly |
| safe | safely | helpful | helpfully |
| equal | equally | careful | carefully |
| happy | happily | lucky | luckily |
| easy | easily | busy | busily |
| late | lately | useful | usefully |
| sudden | suddenly | usual | usually |

When an adjective ends with *-y*, this letter changes to *i* before *-ly* is added (*happy, happily; easy, easily*).

Also notice that some of the adjectives end with the letter *l* (*equal, careful*). Always retain this final *l* when you add *-ly* to form the adverb (*equally, carefully*).

Be careful with the spelling of the adverb *truly*. The final *e* of the adjective *true* is dropped when the suffix *-ly* is added.

■ **6 b   Adverbs That Tell *How***

Many of the adverbs that end with *-ly* tell *how* something is done. Here are some sentences that show this use of adverbs ending with *-ly*. Notice that adverbs can come *before* or *after* the verbs they modify.

He **carefully** polished the old silver bowl.

Ellen and her mom walked **slowly** to their car.

She **easily** finished the test before anyone else.

We **seriously** considered leaving before the storm began.

The students read **quietly** in the library.

Adverbs can also tell the specific *way* in which something is accomplished.

The whole house is heated **electrically**.

The machines **automatically** repeated the same process.

The pottery was **mechanically** produced.

## ■  6 c    Adverbs That Tell *When*

Many adverbs tell something about **time**. These words can let us know *when* something happened or *how often* it happened.

Most adverbs in this group do *not* end with *-ly*. Some of these words can be used as other parts of speech in other situations. In order to use these words as *adverbs*, we need to know how they relate to the verb of the sentence. Here are some adverbs that tell about time or frequency:

| | | | |
|---|---|---|---|
| now | before | once | tomorrow |
| then | after | always | often |
| today | yesterday | never | sometimes |

The following sentences use some of these adverbs of time:

We will go to the zoo **tomorrow**.

**Sometimes** we find arrowheads in the field.

I **often** go to my friend's house after school.

We **always** take a shortcut to get home.

### ■ 6 d    Adverbs That Tell *Where*

There are a number of adverbs that indicate **place**. They tell *where* something is located or they indicate *direction*. Here are some of these adverbs we use very often:

| | | | |
|---|---|---|---|
| up | here | across | upstairs |
| down | there | around | downstairs |
| in | over | backward | inside |
| out | under | forward | outside |

These sentences use some of the adverbs listed above:

My weight always goes **up** after Thanksgiving.

Put the books **here** on this table.

They walked **outside** to look at the storm damage.

I left my coat **upstairs**.

### ■ 6 e    The Location of Adverbs in the Sentence

When adverbs are used to tell *where* and *when* something happens, the order of words must follow the same pattern when these adverbs come after the verb: first tell *where*, then tell *when*.

I go **there often**.

They should be **here soon**.

You would not say "I go often there" or "They should be soon here."

On the other hand, adverbs the tell *how* something is done can usually be placed in a number of locations within the sentence. Look again at two of the sentences you saw earlier in this chapter:

He **carefully** polished the old silver bowl.

Ellen and her mom walked **slowly** to their car.

Notice the change in effect when the adverbs are placed in different locations in these sentences:

**Carefully** he polished the old silver bowl.
He polished the old silver bowl **carefully**.

**Slowly** Ellen and her mom walked to their car.
Ellen and her mom walked to their car **slowly**.

You may want to use the adverb as the first word in the sentence in order to emphasize the way in which something is done: the reader can see that this is an important piece of information. When the adverb appears later in the sentence, it is usually less prominent and simply adds information about how or where or when something was done. This is very different from the situation encountered in the use of the **adjective**, which usually should be placed close to the word it modifies in order to avoid confusion.

# Using Adverbs to Modify Adjectives

Look at these sentences. Arrows point from each adverb (written in boldface) to the word it modifies (in italics).

That was a **very** *good* meal.

We traveled on an **extremely** *slow* boat.

The wind was **unusually** *strong* last night.

In these sentences the adverbs do not modify verbs. Instead, they tell us more about the adjectives *good*, *slow*, and *strong*.

## ■ 6 f    Intensifiers: Adverbs That Tell *How Much*

One group of adverbs is often used to modify adjectives, although some of them can modify verbs or other adverbs as well. These are the adverbs that tell *how much*. They are called **intensifiers** because they add greater *intensity* or emphasis to the words they modify. Here are some frequently used intensifiers:

| | | |
|---|---|---|
| very | too | completely |
| quite | really | entirely |
| hardly | rather | extremely |
| partly | nearly | definitely |

One of the most frequently used adverbs in this group is the word *very*, which often modifies adjectives. In Section **5g** we pointed out that

**6**

you could use this word to see if the following word was an adjective.

There was a *large* hole in the road.

There was a **very** *large* hole in the road.

Also notice that *too* is an adverb that often precedes an adjective. Only *too* can be used this way (not *to* or *two*).

He tried to carry *many* packages.

He tried to carry **too** *many* packages.

In the following examples you first see a sentence in which an adjective modifies a noun. Then an adverb is added to make the adjective more emphatic.

There was a *bad* storm last night.

There was an **extremely** *bad* storm last night.

We were *exhausted* after the long hike.

We were **completely** *exhausted* after the long hike.

The boat was *damaged* in the storm.

The boat was **heavily** *damaged* in the storm.

As you can see in these examples, adverbs are often used to modify *predicate adjectives* that come after linking verbs.

# Using Adverbs to Modify Other Adverbs

Look at the words connected by arrows in these sentences:

We walked **slowly**. We walked **very slowly**.

I heard him **clearly**. I heard him **quite clearly**.

They played **well**. They played **extremely well**.

The first sentence in each pair contains an adverb that modifies a verb. The second sentence in each pair adds *another* adverb which intensifies the first adverb.

# Using Adverbs Correctly

■ **6 g**    Using *good* and *well*

The words *good* and *well* seem to mean much the same thing, but they must be used carefully because there are important differences between them. Much depends on the type of verb used in the sentence.

---

• *Good* is often an adjective which may precede a noun.

We had a **good** time.

That was a very **good** movie.

• *Good* may also be used as a predicate adjective following **linking verbs** such as *feel* or *look* or *taste*.

This soup tastes **good**.

Your new jacket looks very **good**.

---

• *Well* is often used as an adverb to modify a verb by telling *how* something is done. This is especially true when *well* is used in sentences with an **action verb**.

The team played very **well**.

This author writes **well**.

---

Now look at some sentences using *well* and *good*. Notice the kind of verb used in each case.

How do you feel? I feel *good*. I am *well*.

Here the words *good* and *well* are both **adjectives**. In fact, they are predicate adjectives that follow the linking verbs *feel* and *am*. Each adjective defines the subject, *I*.

Notice how *well* and *good* are used in these sentences:

How was Ed's speech? His speech was *good*. He spoke **well**.

Here the adjective *good* modifies the subject *speech* in the second sentence. However, the word *well* is an adverb that modifies the verb *spoke* in the third sentence. It does not tell about the speech itself; it tells *how* Ed spoke.

What do you think about the next sentences? Do they use *good* and *well* correctly?

This coat looks very *good*. It fits very **well**.

The structure of these sentences seems to be the same. They both begin with a subject and a verb followed by the words *very good* or *very well*. Shouldn't the second sentence read "It fits very *good*"?

You can figure this out if you notice the kind of **verb** used in each sentence. In the first sentence, the linking verb *looks* simply connects the subject *coat* with the predicate adjective *good*. This adjective describes how the coat *appears*, not what it does. This sentence is correctly written.

In the second sentence, the word *fits* tells what the coat *does*. The adverb *well* tells how the coat fits; it does not describe the appearance of the coat. This sentence is also written correctly.

The following guidelines will help you use *good* and *well* correctly:

- *Good* is often used as an adjective, but it should not be used as an adverb. When you want to modify a noun or a pronoun, use the adjective *good*.

  That was a *good* movie.

- *Well* is often used as an adverb to tell *how* something is done. *Well* is used as an adverb after an **action verb**. Always modify a verb with the adverb *well*, not the adjective *good*.

  The team played very *well*.

- *Well* can be used as an adjective to describe how something *is* or how someone *feels*. The adjective *well* means that things are in satisfactory condition or that a person is in good health and is not ill. *Well* is used as an adjective after a **linking verb**.

  All was *well* after the storm passed.

  I don't feel very *well* today.

## ■ 6 h   Making Comparisons with Adverbs

In Chapter 5 of this book you saw that adjectives could be used to compare two things or more than two things. Adverbs can be used in the same way.

Ellen runs **fast**, but Joan runs **faster**. Susan runs **fastest** of all.

Each of these boldfaced words tells how someone *runs*. The adverb *fast* is used in its base form and in other forms that show differing degrees of speed (*faster*, *fastest*).

### • Adverbs in the Positive Degree

Adverbs can be used in the **positive degree**. This is the basic form of the word that modifies a single verb or adverb or adjective. Notice that adverbs in the positive degree often involve a suffix such as *-ly*.

**6**

They ran **quickly** across the street.

This is an **extremely** interesting book.

He worked **hard** on his test.

- **Adverbs in the Comparative Degree**

Adverbs can be used to compare two actions. With some adverbs, the **comparative degree** adds *er* to the end of the base word, just as adjectives did. Usually *er* is added to adverbs that contain one syllable in the positive degree.

He worked **harder** than I did for the test.

We will arrive **sooner** than they will.

Many adverbs end with *-ly* or contain two or three syllables. For this reason, we usually add the word *more* before the adverb in order to make comparisons.

She swims **more skillfully** than I do.

We must plan **more carefully** for our next trip.

- **Adverbs in the Superlative Degree**

In order to compare more than two actions, adverbs are used in the **superlative degree**. A few adverbs can add the inflection *est* to the base word. These are usually the adverbs that contain one syllable in the positive degree.

They worked the **hardest** of anybody.

This tree grows the **tallest** of all those in the forest.

With most adverbs of two or more syllables, we add the word *most* to show the superlative degree.

I saw the **most cleverly** drawn cartoons yesterday.

This is the **most beautifully** written book of all.

There are a few adverbs that do not fit the patterns discussed above. Here are the forms of these irregular adverbs:

| Positive | Comparative | Superlative |
|----------|-------------|-------------|
| well | better | (the) best |
| badly | worse | (the) worst |
| far | farther | farthest |
| little | less | least |

Ralph played **well**, but Juan played even **better**.
Kim played **best** of all.

We traveled **far** to reach our destination, but they traveled **farther** than we did.

## ■ 6 i  Words That Can Be Adjectives or Adverbs

In Section **6g** you saw that the word *well* could be an adverb when it described how something was *done*. *Well* is usually used as an adverb after an *action verb*.

She played **well**.

The word *well* can also be an adjective when it describes what something *is* or how someone *feels*. *Well* is usually used as an adjective after a *linking verb*.

She felt **well**.

There are other words that can be adjectives or adverbs, depending on their use in the sentence. The spelling of the word does not change, but its relationship to other words does.

The word *hard* is a good example. Look at these sentences:

Ellen and Tom work **hard**. (**adverb**)

This bench is *hard*. (*adjective*)

In the first sentence, the adverb *hard* describes how Ellen and Tom *work*. In the second sentence, the predicate adjective *hard* describes what the bench *is*.

The following examples contain words that can be adjectives or adverbs, depending on their function in the sentence. The first sentence of each pair contains an **adverb** (written in boldface). In the second sentence of each pair, the same word serves as an *adjective* (written in italics).

The plane arrived **early**.
We took an *early* plane from Chicago.

The team practiced **late** into the evening.
There is a *late* bus that leaves in an hour.

We worked **long** and diligently to finish the job.
We need a *long* board to replace the damaged one.

The plane flew **low** across the field.
There is a *low* bridge up ahead.

### ■ 6 j   Avoiding Double Negatives: The Adverb *not*

The word *not* is an adverb, and it is also a *negative* word. This means that it is used to deny or refuse something or to say that something happened "in no way" or "to no degree."

You know that *not* often follows a verb directly.

I **do not** know where he is.

We **are not** leaving until noon.

They **have not** finished the job yet.

We also often use contractions to combine *not* with the verb that precedes it.

I **don't** know where he is.

We **aren't** leaving until noon.

They **haven't** finished the job yet.

Whenever the adverb *not* is used in a sentence, there should be no other negative words in that sentence. Here is a list of some of the most familiar negative words. After each negative word you see the positive form of that word.

| Negative | Positive | Negative | Positive |
|----------|----------|----------|----------|
| no | any | no one | anyone |
| hardly | almost | nobody | anybody |
| none | any | nowhere | anywhere |
| never | ever | nothing | anything |

If *not* is used along with another negative word in a sentence, then the two words tend to cancel each other. This is called the **double negative**. Here are a few sentences that contain double negatives:

I **do not** have *no* more money.

He **could not** find *none* of his books.

You **should not** give *nothing* to them.

Because *not* has already established the negative, it is confusing to use still another word that has a negative meaning. Instead, we should use the *positive* form of the words in italics. Here is the way the preceding sentences should be written:

I **do not** have *any* more money.

He **could not** find *any* of his books.

You **should not** give *anything* to them.

### ■ 6 k    Watching for Mistakes

Is there anything wrong with this sentence?

Ed and Bill raced each other. Bill ran the **fastest**.

Only two people are being compared, but the second sentence uses the superlative degree of the adverb *fast* to tell how Ed and Bill *ran*. This should not be used to compare only two things. Instead, the second sentence should say, "Bill ran **faster** than Ed."

Here is another sentence that makes a comparison. What is wrong with it?

I tasted four of the baloney sandwiches, and this one tasted **worse** of all.

This sentence compares four things, but it uses the adverb *worse* in the comparative degree. Because we are comparing more than two things, the adverb should be *worst*, which is the superlative degree.

Be careful with adjectives and adverbs when you make comparisons. Remember that the superlative form is used when you compare *more* than two things. It is especially important to watch for the words *worse* (comparative) and *worst* (superlative).

The words *real* and *really* must also be used carefully. Here are some sentences using the word *real*.

This is made of *real* gold. It is not an imitation.

The story told about *real* life. It was not fiction.

In these sentences the adjective *real* is used to modify the nouns *gold* and *life*. Always use *real* when you need an adjective to modify a noun.

The next two sentences use the word *really:*

I did not *really* believe everything he said.

That story was *really* interesting.

In the first sentence the adverb *really* modifies the verb *believe*. In the last sentence, the adverb *really* modifies the adjective *interesting*. We should use the adverb *really* here—not the adjective *real*—to modify verbs and adjectives.

You can see that the adverb *really* is formed by adding the suffix *-ly* to the adjective *real*. The important thing is to use these two words in their proper places. Be sure to use *real* as an adjective to modify a noun. Use *really* when you need an adverb to modify a verb, an adjective, or another adverb.

Sometimes you may hear statements like these, or you may say or write things like this yourself:

That movie was **real** *funny*.

Those hot dogs tasted **real** *good*.

It took a **real** *long* time to make the trip.

In these sentences, the adjectives *funny* and *good* and *long* modify the nouns *movie* and *hot dogs* and *time*. However, these adjectives are preceded by another adjective, *real*. You know that this is not correct because only **adverbs** should modify adjectives. The word *really* should be used in these sentences.

That movie was **really** *funny*.

Those hot dogs tasted **really** *good*.

It took a **really** *long* time to make the trip.

## ■ 6 1    Using Adverbs in Sentences

It is possible to use several adverbs in a single sentence.

These flowers will **probably** wither away **soon**.

My coat is **extremely** damp. It is **slowly** drying **downstairs** in the basement.

The following sentences were written by students your age. Look at the adverbs written in boldface and find the words that are modified by each of these adverbs.

**Suddenly** there was a flash of light and when the air **finally** cleared she saw a gorgeous prince that looked just like Tom Cruise. The girl was **very** happy so she went with him and lived **happily** ever after.

It was sunny so he got to play **outside** with his friends.

We hope you don't mind this little mess. It's not **extremely** big.

My dad works **hard** as an attorney.

We **finally** got things under control.

In the morning, Batman gets up **early** and goes **downstairs** to do his chores. **Then** he chases bad guys and **finally** catches them.

I hope **someday** my wish will come true.

I have to go to school **tomorrow**, not **today**.

**6**

# *Check Your Understanding*

## Adverbs that Modify Verbs, Adjectives, and Adverbs
*Answers begin on p. 283.*

**1.** Change the word in parentheses to an **adverb** and draw an arrow from the adverb to the **verb** it modifies.

1. He ran (quick) toward us.
2. We watched him very (careful).
3. They (usual) leave home at seven-thirty.
4. The storm blew up (sudden) from the west.
5. We trudged (slow) through the mud.

**2.** Underline the **adverb** in each sentence and draw an arrow from the adverb to the **adjective** it modifies.

1. This turned out to be an unusually difficult job.

2. That movie was completely ridiculous.

3. We waited an extremely long time for the bus.

4. There was a very large tree lying across the road.

5. The stone was too heavy for us to move.

**3.** Draw an arrow from the adverb in boldface to the word it modifies. Then indicate whether the *modified word* is a verb, an adjective, or another adverb. Here is an example:

They walked **very** slowly back to the bus. (adverb)

1. The missing watch appeared **unexpectedly**.

2. Isn't it **unusually** early to be leaving for school?

3. They played **extremely** well in the last game.

4. The **slightly** damaged books were on sale at low prices.

# *Check Your Understanding*

### Using Adverbs Correctly

**1.** Choose the correct word from those given in parentheses.

    1. Did they play as (good, well) as you hoped they would?
    2. We traveled (farther, farthest) than they did.
    3. The movie was (real, really) enjoyable.
    4. I didn't find (none, any) of the books you wanted.
    5. She sang very (good, well) in the concert.

**2.** In these sentences, adverbs are written in the positive degree (in parentheses). Use the adverb in the **comparative** or **superlative** degree, as required.

    1. This kite flies much (good) than that one.
    2. I believe this is the (unusual) fossil in the museum.
    3. This skateboard runs much (bad) than the other one.
    4. I hope this test is (easy) than the last one.
    5. This was judged the (beautiful) flower in the show.

**3.** Correct the mistake you find in each sentence.

    1. We didn't see nobody we knew.
    2. He's the worse baseball player I ever saw.
    3. My brother is taller than I am, but I can run fastest.
    4. There wasn't nothing we could do about it.
    5. I thought they did a real good job.

# 7

# Function Words: Prepositions and Conjunctions

In earlier chapters we looked at words that had definite meanings of their own. Nouns and pronouns *named* things, verbs often expressed *actions*, and adjectives and adverbs *modified* other words. Almost all the words in any dictionary are nouns, verbs, adjectives, or adverbs. They are the **vocabulary words** that allow us to talk about a wide variety of subjects. They are like the boards and bricks used to build a house.

In this chapter we will look at parts of speech that serve as **function words** within the sentence.

---

**Function words** (also called **structure words**) do *not* name things or express actions. However, they are extremely important because they make *connections* and show *relationships* among other parts of speech.

---

If vocabulary words are like the boards and bricks used to build a house, then function words are like the nails and mortar that hold the boards and bricks together. Function words provide guideposts and directional signals that allow us to arrange vocabulary words into meaningful patterns called *sentences*. Although there aren't very many function words, they are used more frequently than are any other words in the English language.

Now we will look at one type of function word that is used in almost every sentence: the **preposition**.

# Prepositions

Can you make sense of these groups of words?

> I met them ___ the mall. We looked ___ the store windows for a while. Then we went ___ a movie.

There is nothing wrong with the order of words, and you can probably guess which words are missing. However, in order for these sentences to be completely clear, we need to add the words *at*, *in*, and *to*. These words are **prepositions.**

> • **Prepositions** show how *nouns* and *pronouns* are related to other words in the sentence.

We can define nouns such as *table* or *house* by describing characteristics that everyone can see. However, it is much more difficult to define prepositions. In fact, if you look for words such as *of* or *to* in a large dictionary, you often find that they are first labeled as *function words* and then described in terms of what they *do* within the sentence.

## ■ 7 a    The Most Important Prepositions

Here are some of the prepositions that you use very often:

| | | |
|---|---|---|
| about | beyond | over |
| above | by | past |
| across | down | since |
| after | during | through |
| against | except | to |
| along | for | toward |
| around | from | under |
| at | in | until |
| before | into | up |
| behind | like | upon |
| below | of | with |
| beside | off | within |
| between | on | without |

Prepositions are often used just before nouns or pronouns: "*to* me," "*for* Susan," or "*with* you," for example. Sometimes adjectives appear between the preposition and the noun: "*up* the big hill" or "*with* my best friend." Now we will see why such groups of words are important.

## ■ 7 b    Using Prepositions in the Sentence

The meaning of the sentence can be greatly affected by the choice of prepositions. Look at this group of words, for example:

He looked ___ his car.

When we use a variety of prepositions in the blank space, we can write sentences that have very different meanings.

He looked **at** his car.

He looked **for** his car.

He looked **behind** his car.

He looked **under** his car.

He looked **inside** his car.

In each sentence, the preposition (in boldface) shows the relationship between the noun *car* and the rest of the sentence. This relationship changes in every sentence because the preposition changes, even as the other words remain the same.

Now look at some more sentences that use prepositions.

Please give these books **to** her.

I am going **with** her next Saturday.

This package must be **for** her.

Here the prepositions show the relationship of the pronoun *her*, to the rest of the sentence. Although the pronoun *her* remains the same, the connection to the other words changes.

The next sentences were written by students your age. The prepositions are printed in boldface.

He tried to run, but he got stuck **in** a big puddle **of** tar.

We had to write a report **about** the Sahara Desert.

Sometimes he rides **to** school **with** me.

Batman lives **in** an old house, but the Batcave is **in** an abandoned mine. **In** the morning he sometimes goes **into** town **for** some things.

As you can see, each preposition is followed by a noun or pronoun (*of tar; with me*). Sometimes other words appear before the noun (*in a big puddle; for some things*). Now we will look at the patterns formed by prepositions and the nouns or pronouns that follow them.

### ■ 7 c  Prepositional Phrases

Here are some groups of words taken from sentences you have just seen:

> behind his car
>
> to school
>
> in the morning
>
> into town
>
> with her
>
> about the Sahara Desert

Each of these examples is a **prepositional phrase**.

---

- A **phrase** is a group of two or more related words which form *part* of a sentence. A phrase can express a single thought, but a phrase cannot form a complete sentence because it does *not* contain its own subject and predicate. Phrases have meaning only in relation to the rest of the sentence.
- A **prepositional phrase** begins with a preposition and ends with a noun or a pronoun: *with my friends, to them*.

---

## ■ 7 d    The Object of the Preposition

> • The **object of the preposition** is the noun or pronoun that comes at the end of a prepositional phrase. It is the word which the preposition relates to other words in the sentence.

In each of the following prepositional phrases, the object of the preposition is written in boldface:

for **me**

to my **school**

at the **movies**

with **us**

Whenever you write a prepositional phrase that ends with a *pronoun*, remember to use the **object** form of the pronoun.

OBJECT PRONOUNS

|  | Singular | Plural |
|---|---|---|
| **First person:** | me | us |
| **Second person:** | you | you |
| **Third person:** | him | them |
|  | her |  |
|  | it |  |

In the next sentences you see some of these pronouns used as the object of the preposition. Each preposition is written in boldface; each object is written in italics. Remember that object pronouns are used even when another person's name is included as part of the object of the sentence.

Are we going **with** *them*?

They brought some packages **for** *me*.

Did he show his new gloves **to** *you*?

They are still waiting **for** *us.*

They gave some tickets **to** *Jaime and me.*

The letters were **for** *Maria and her.*

In the following sentences you see both nouns *and* pronouns used as objects of prepositions. In fact, most of the sentences contain *two* prepositional phrases.

Some books *in that pile* fell *off the table.*

We took a trip *to Disneyland* last summer.

Be sure to give this note *to her.*

*After* the game we went *to our friend's house.*

He is waiting *in the shop* *around* the corner.

These books were *on the table* *beside* the desk.

I am going *to a movie* *with* my friends.

We have received two letters *from* him *since* November.

Notice the prepositional phrase *off the table* in the first sentence. When you use *off* as a preposition, it is not necessary to follow it with the preposition *of.*

He fell *off* his bike. (**NOT** He fell *off of* his bike.)

In some sentences you saw groups of words such as *to run* and *to give.* These were not marked as prepositional phrases even though they began with the word *to.* This is because the word following *to* is a **verb** in these examples. *To run* and *to give* are not prepositional phrases because they do not end with a noun or pronoun. These words make up a particular verb form called the **infinitive**. You will learn about infinitives in Section **8n**.

## ■ 7 e    Prepositional Phrases Used as Adjectives

Look at the two sentences given below. The words in italics are examples of **adjective phrases**. This term identifies prepositional phrases that are used as adjectives.

The stamps *in this album* are very valuable.

The library *in my school* has books *about space travel*.

The following diagram of the first sentence shows the subject, the verb, and the predicate adjective written on the base line. This diagram also shows how the prepositional phrase *in this album* relates to the subject of the sentence, *stamps*. Notice how the words which modify the subject (as well as the predicate adjective) are written below the base line.

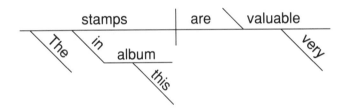

## ■ 7 f    Prepositional Phrases Used as Adverbs

Look at the use of prepositional phrases in these sentences:

We left **before** *the storm*.

I found my boots **in** *the attic*.

We climbed the steep hill **with** *great difficulty*.

The words in italics are called **adverb phrases**. This term identifies prepositional phrases that are used as adverbs.

In the first sentence, the phrase *before the storm* tells *when* something happened. In the next sentence, the phrase *in the attic* tells *where* something was found. In the last sentence, the phrase *with great difficulty* tells *how* something was done.

In the next example, the second sentence is more informative than the first sentence because we have used a prepositional phrase that tells more about the verb.

I met my friends.
I met my friends **after** school.

The following diagram shows how the prepositional phrase *after school* is used as an adverb to modify the verb *met*.

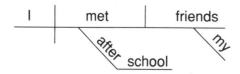

In Chapter 6 of this book you saw that adverbs can modify adjectives or other adverbs as well as verbs. The same is true when a prepositional phrase is used as an adverb. Here is a sentence in which a prepositional phrase functions as an adverb that modifies an adjective:

The dress is blue **with** white trim.

The predicate adjective *blue* tells the color of the dress, and the prepositional phrase *with white trim* tells even more about the adjective *blue*.

The next sentence uses a prepositional phrase as an adverb to modify another adverb.

They left late **in** the afternoon.

The adverb *late* tells when they left, and the phrase *in the afternoon* also functions as an adverb that gives even more information about the word *late*.

■ **7 g    The Location of Prepositional Phrases in the Sentence**

Be careful when you use a prepositional phrase between the subject and the verb in a sentence. Sometimes the word before the verb may *appear* to be the subject even though it is not. The next sentence contains the kind of mistake that can slip by when you use a prepositional phrase between the subject and the verb.

The list *of all the books* **are** very long.

The word *books* appears just before the verb. If you thought that the plural noun *books* was the subject, you would use the plural verb *are*.

However, *books* is actually the object of the preposition *of*; the subject of the sentence is the word *list*. This singular subject should be matched with a singular verb.

The list *of all the books* **is** very long.

When you diagram this sentence, you see that the singular verb *is* logically follows the singular noun *list*.

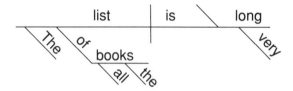

If sentences are going to make sense, then each prepositional phrase should relate clearly to the word it modifies. This is especially true when prepositional phrases are used as *adjectives*. When prepositional phrases stray too far from the words they modify, sentences can become confusing.

The man drove the bus *in the green uniform*.

It is not likely that the bus was wearing a green uniform, but this sentence makes it look that way. The prepositional phrase *in the green uniform* is intended to function as an adjective modifying *The man*.

The man *in the green uniform* drove the bus.

Look at the following sentences, written by a student in the middle grades. Try to find all the prepositional phrases for yourself. Can you see any problems in the way some of the phrases are used?

After a hard day's work. My dad comes home and helps me with my homework. At six in the morning. He goes to his job until nine at night.

The very first prepositional phrase, "After a hard day's work," is written to look like a sentence, but a *phrase* cannot be a sentence because it does not have its own subject and predicate. The first phrase should be written so that it forms the beginning of a complete sentence:

*After* a hard day's work, my dad comes home and helps me with my homework.

Now the opening prepositional phrase clearly functions as an adverb phrase that tells *when* dad comes home. Notice that "with my homework" is also a prepositional phrase.

The same thing happens with the next two phrases and the sentence that follows. These should be connected to show that the prepositional phrases "At six / in the morning" form the beginning of a complete sentence. The end of the sentence is correct.

**At** *six* **in** *the morning*, he goes to his job until nine at night.

Each of the phrases written in italics should be connected to the complete sentence that follows it, and the comma should be used to show that there is more to come after the phrases.

There are three more prepositional phrases in the last sentence:

to his job    until nine    at night

These phrases function as adverbs that tell *where* and *when* dad goes.

### ■ 7.h    Ending Sentences with a Preposition

The word *preposition* originated in a Latin verb meaning "to put something *in front of* something else." When the principles of English grammar were being developed in past centuries, the meaning of the word *preposition* was taken literally. It was considered to be "a word that must be placed *in front of* its object." This is the way prepositions are usually used, and this is the way we have studied them so far.

In spite of the literal meaning of the word, the important thing is for prepositions to be used in ways that make the sentence clear. In some cases, this means that prepositions may be more effectively used *after* their objects. Sometimes it is awkward to construct prepositional phrases exactly according to the principles set down in the past. You can see this in the following sentences, which are technically correct but seem very stiff and formal to us:

**About** *what* was he talking?

This is the book **for** *which* I was looking.

This is material **with** *which* it is easy to work.

**Of** *how many* examples can you think?

In everyday conversation and writing, we would probably place the preposition at the *end* of each sentence:

What was he talking *about*?

This is the book I was looking *for*.

This material is easy to work *with*.

How many examples can you think *of*?

Even though the prepositions come at the end and their objects come at the beginning, these sentences are preferable to the earlier sentences that placed each preposition before its object. If the sentence is more clear with the preposition at the end, then this structure is acceptable.

Most of the time you can avoid using the preposition at the end of the sentence if you take care to place the complete prepositional phrase near the word it modifies. Sometimes sentences can be completely rewritten to make them more clear:

What was the subject *of the speech?*

It is easy to work *with this material.*

Can you think *of other examples?*

Questions that begin with *wh-* words often place the preposition at the end. Here are a few examples:

*What* were they talking *about?*

*Which* books are you looking *for?*

*Whom* were you talking *to?*

*Whom* was she waiting *for?*

The last two sentences bring up another question concerning the use of prepositions. Ideally, these sentences should be written and spoken this way:

*To whom* were you talking?

*For whom* was she waiting?

Now these sentences are completely clear because each preposition has been placed directly before its object. However, there is another consideration that is more important than the location of the preposition. This is the use of the pronoun *whom*, which is the only word that can function as the *object* of each preposition.

Look at the same sentences as they might be written or spoken in everyday conversation:

*Who* were you talking **to**?

*Who* was she waiting **for**?

Now these sentences are **not** correct because the subject pronoun *who* begins each sentence. A *subject* pronoun cannot be the *object* of the preposition. Furthermore, the subjects of these sentences are the words *you* and *she*. For these reasons, only the object pronoun *whom* should be used, no matter where the preposition is placed.

# Conjunctions

Supply the missing words in this sentence:

I met them __ the mall, ___ we went __ a movie.

You know that the first missing word (*at*) and the last one (*to*) are prepositions. The other missing word, *and*, connects the two parts of this compound sentence. It is a member of another important group of function words that we use every day. You will see some of these function words written in boldface in the following sentences.

Mom **and** I ran into Susan **and** Ellen at the store.

I like to play baseball **and** football.

We swam **and** played volleyball **and** got some sun.

I wanted to go outside **but** it was raining too hard.

They were tired **but** very happy after they won the game.

We left early, **but** they stayed until the end of the movie.

We can leave now **or** wait for them to arrive.

Does he play right field **or** center field?

Words such as *and*, *but*, and *or* are **conjunctions**. They are among the most frequently used words in the English language. Their principal reason for existence is to allow us to arrange other words into meaningful patterns.

> • **Conjunctions** are function words that *join* two or more words, phrases, or other parts of sentences.

These function words can be used in several ways within the sentence. We will look now at the three most important types of conjunctions.

## ■ 7 i    Coordinating Conjunctions

The words *and*, *but*, and *or* are examples of coordinating conjunctions.

> • **Coordinating conjunctions** are words that can be used to connect other words such as nouns or verbs. They can also be used to show the relationship between parts of the sentence.

When we *coordinate* things, we cause them to work well *together*. Often the things that we coordinate are of equal importance within the sentence.

On the next page you will see three of the ways in which the coordinating conjunction *and* may be used.

---

*And* is used to *join* words or groups of words. This word is often used to connect the words in *compound subjects* and *compound predicates*.

*Bill* **and** *I* are on the same team.

We *practice* after school **and** *play* on Saturdays.

---

*And* often connects the parts of a *compound sentence*. Remember that a **comma** is usually placed before the conjunction in a compound sentence.

We left early in the morning, **and** we got there before dark.

The parade begins at noon, **and** the game starts at one.

---

*And* can be used to connect words in a series.

We found old shoes **and** hats **and** junk in the attic.

Our picnic was enjoyed by zillions of ants **and** flies **and** gnats.

---

The coordinating conjunctions *but* and *or* show other kinds of connections between words.

---

*But* is used to show *contrast*. It can show that two words or groups of words are different from each other.

We felt tired **but** happy when the trip was over.

The package was small **but** very heavy.

---

*But* can also connect the parts of a compound sentence.

They like to swim, **but** I prefer to go fishing.

This looks old and shabby, **but** it is very valuable.

---

*Or* is used to show that there is a *choice* between different things.

> You can have chocolate **or** strawberry ice cream.

> Mom **or** dad should know when they're coming back.

This word can also connect the parts of a compound sentence.

> We can wait for them, **or** we can ask mom pick us up.

The words *yet*, *for*, and *nor* can also be used as coordinating conjunctions. In this case, the word *yet* means much the same as *but*, and *for* means "the reason is that." *Nor* is used to connect parts of *negative* sentences.

> The car was old and rusty, **yet** it ran very well.

> They will probably succeed, **for** they have worked hard and prepared well.

> I haven't seen him today, **nor** do I expect to see him tomorrow.

## ■ 7 j  Subordinating Conjunctions

Look at the words written in italics in these sentences, and notice how they relate to the first part of each sentence. Pay close attention to the word in boldface in each sentence.

> Be sure to pick up the clothes **before** *the store closes*.

> We were eager to leave **after** *the storm ended*.

> They decided to wait **because** *the snow was so heavy*.

> She visits her grandparents **whenever** *she can*.

The words in boldface are used as **subordinating conjunctions** in these sentences.

**7**

> • **Subordinating conjunctions** are words that connect the main part of a sentence with another part which serves as a modifier. The words that follow the subordinating conjunction make sense only in relation to the main part of the sentence.

When you saw groups of words such as *before the store closes* and *after the storm ended*, you could tell that these words were not complete in themselves. They became important only when you related them to the rest of the sentence. Each group of words was introduced by a *subordinating conjunction*.

Here are some subordinating conjunctions that are often used:

| | | |
|---|---|---|
| after | if | until |
| although | since | when |
| as | than | whenever |
| because | though | where |
| before | unless | while |

In Section **9n** you will learn more about how to use subordinating conjunctions to introduce groups of words that depend on the main part of the sentence for their meaning.

■ **7 k    Correlative Conjunctions**

The word *correlate* means "to show a connection between things." The function of correlative conjunctions is similar to the function of coordinating conjunctions. However, there is one important thing you should notice about correlative conjunctions. Look at the following sentences and see how these conjunctions are used:

**If** they get here in time, **then** we can go to the movie.

**Both** Juan **and** Kim were in the school play.

**Either** Nancy **or** Frank will meet you after school.

**Neither** I **nor** my friends knew where to look.

He left **not only** his books **but also** his gloves on the bus.

> • **Correlative conjunctions** are always used in pairs. They show the relationship between one part of a sentence and another part of the sentence.

Here are the most frequently used correlative conjunctions:

**if . . . then**

**both . . . and**

**either . . . or**

**neither . . . nor**

**not only . . . but also**

---

*If* you use the first part of a correlative conjunction, *then* you must follow it with the second part of the pattern.

---

## ■ 71 Agreement of Verbs with Compound Subjects

We have seen that the coordinating conjunction *and* can be used to join simple subjects to form a compound subject.

My friend **and** I *are* in the same class.

It is also possible to use the correlative conjunction *both . . . and* to join parts of a compound subject.

**Both** Maria **and** Susan were in the play.

---

Whenever *and* or *both . . . and* are used to join words in a compound subject, *the verb is **always plural**.*

---

On the other hand, the coordinating conjunction *or* can be used to join two or more simple subjects into a compound subject. You can also use the correlative conjunctions *either . . . or* or *neither . . . nor* to join the parts of a compound subject. When you use compound subjects involving these conjunctions, some sentences will require a singular verb while

**7**

other sentences will require a plural verb. You must look carefully at the subject of each sentence in order to see which form of the verb to use.

---

Whenever *or* or *nor* is used to join parts of a compound subject, *the verb matches the simple subject that is* **closest to it**.

---

These sentences show how to decide on the verb form to use:

My mom **or** my sister *is* at home now.

His dad **or** his brothers *are* always at every game.

**Either** this book **or** those magazines *contain* the information you need.

**Neither** the cars **nor** the bus *was* able to get through the snow.

# *Check Your Understanding*

## Prepositions

*Answers begin on p. 285.*

1.  Draw one line under each complete prepositional phrase. Add a second line under the *preposition* itself. Here is an example:

    After school we walked through the park.

    1.  The scientists looked for the source of the radiation.
    2.  This novel by Dickens is set in England and in France.
    3.  Answers to your questions are in one chapter of this book.
    4.  Your gloves are on the chair beside the window.
    5.  For several years we have gone to the beach on vacation.

2.  Underline each complete prepositional phrase. Draw an arrow from the phrase to the word it modifies. Also indicate which phrases function as **adjectives** and which phrases function as **adverbs**. Here is an example:

    The chairs in the backyard need painting.  (adjective)

    1.  I raked the lawn before dark.
    2.  The books on this shelf are all biographies.
    3.  Please put this coat in the closet.
    4.  After the game we went out to get pizza.
    5.  The house across the street is being painted.

3.  Make the necessary corrections in the following sentences. You may need to change the location of some prepositional phrases, or you may need to change the verb when a prepositional phrase is used after the subject. After you have corrected each sentence, underline each prepositional phrase.

    1.  Four of the students have baby sisters in my class.
    2.  The best one of these drinks are the grape soda.
    3.  We looked for boots in three stores with rubber soles.
    4.  Some kids in my school is on a little league team.

# *Check Your Understanding*

## Conjunctions

**1.** The following sentences can be combined by using the **coordinating conjunctions** *and, or,* or *but* to form compound subjects, compound predicates, or compound sentences.

> Carlos looked for his ticket. He found it under the desk.
> Carlos looked for his ticket, **and** he found it under the desk.

1. Ellen brought some colored leaves to class. Maria brought some colored leaves to class.
2. We looked in a dozen magazines. We didn't find the kind of photograph we wanted.
3. We may go to a movie. We may stay home and watch TV.
4. Jaime likes math. He is very good in science.
5. Kim made some cookies. Sue brought some doughnuts.

**2.** Look for the **subordinating conjunctions** in the following sentences. Underline the complete group of words that begins with each conjunction, and then add a second line beneath the conjunction itself. Here is an example:

> We got completely soaked <u>when the storm began</u>.

1. Because it was raining so hard, we decided to stay inside.
2. He got lost when he made a wrong turn.
3. After we finish shopping, we will get something to drink.
4. Although the weather was bad, we decided to go anyway.
5. I managed to finish the test before the bell rang.

**3.** Look for the **correlative conjunctions** in the following sentences. Underline the two words or groups of words that make up each correlative conjunction. Here is an example:

> <u>If</u> the game ends early, <u>then</u> we can get back before dark.

1. Please bring either my raincoat or my umbrella.
2. Both my sister and my aunt have birthdays this month.
3. If you find a good photograph of the Grand Canyon, then please let me see it.
4. He has neither cleaned his room nor finished his homework.
5. The house was damaged not only by the wind but also by the flood.

# 8

# More about Verbs

In Chapter 4 we began to look at verbs. Now we will learn more about how to use verbs in sentences.

## Using Action Verbs

You know that many verbs express actions. In Section **4c** you saw that action verbs may be followed by a **direct object** that receives the action of the verb. It is also possible to use many action verbs *without* a direct object. These two ways of using action verbs are so important that they have special names of their own.

### ■ 8 a   Transitive Verbs

Look at the following sentences. Each action verb is written in italics and each direct object is written in boldface.

Who *lifted* all those heavy **boxes**?

The batter *hit* the **ball** over the fence.

We *met* **them** after the game.

I *saw* your **book** lying on the table.

We *cut* all the dead **branches** from the tree.

When action verbs are used this way, they are called **transitive verbs**.

**8**

> • A **transitive verb** is an *action verb* that is followed by a **direct object**. Transitive verbs carry the action from the subject to the direct object.

The action expressed by a transitive verb is completed by the direct object. This object tells *who* or *what* receives the action of the verb. Some verbs would not make sense without a direct object. If you saw sentences that began with the following words, you would immediately expect more information.

I threw . . .

We saw . . .

They pushed . . .

She brought . . .

He lifted . . .

These words will not make sense until a **direct object** is supplied: *What* did you throw? *What* or *whom* did we see?

### ■ 8 b    Intransitive Verbs

Although many action verbs *are* often followed by direct objects, this is not the only way that action verbs can be used. Some action verbs can be used *with* or *without* a direct object.

In the following examples, the first sentence in each pair contains an action verb followed by a direct object. What happens when the same action verb is used in the second sentence of each pair?

I could *hear* the **speaker** very clearly.
I could *hear* very clearly.

They could hardly *see* the broken **step** in the dim light.
They could hardly *see* in the dim light.

The inspectors *searched* the old **warehouse**.
The inspectors *searched* carefully and thoroughly.

This plane *flies* many **passengers**.
This plane *flies* very fast.

In the second sentence of each pair the verb tells that something happens, but there is no direct object. When action verbs are used this way, they are called **intransitive verbs**.

> • An **intransitive verb** is an *action verb* that is **not** followed by a direct object.

Intransitive verbs may be followed by words that tell *when* or *how* an action takes place, but they are not followed by words that answer the question **what?** or **whom?**

We have already seen that some words can belong to more than one part of speech, depending on their use in various sentences. Now we see that many verbs can be *transitive* in one sentence and *intransitive* in another. This is one more example of the flexibility of words in the English language.

There are three pairs of verbs that look and sound very similar. However, one verb in each pair is always *transitive*, while the other is always *intransitive*.

| Transitive | Intransitive |
|---|---|
| set | sit |
| lay | lie |
| raise | rise |

These three pairs of verbs are used in the following sentences. Arrows point from each transitive verb to its direct object.

Please *set* these **books** on the shelf.
Everyone please *sit* down.

*Lay* the **packages** on the table over there.
I need to *lie* down and rest for a while.

Please *raise* the **window**.
I like to watch the sun *rise* every morning.

**8**

Intransitive verbs tell about something that the subject *itself* does. **Transitive verbs** tell us that the action of the verb is received *by* something or someone other than the subject.

> • You can *sit* down yourself, but you *set* an object on the shelf.
> • You can *lie* down and rest yourself, but you *lay* an object on the table.
> • You can *rise* from a chair yourself or you can see the sun itself *rise* in the east, but you *raise* a window or a flag.

## ■ 8 c    Using Indirect Objects with Transitive Verbs

We have seen that *transitive verbs* always take *direct objects*. There is still another kind of object that can be used in sentences that contain transitive verbs.

Look at the following pairs of sentences. The first sentence in each pair contains a transitive verb followed by a direct object. In the second sentence, other words are added in boldface. How do these added words affect the sentence?

Lillian brought a book.
Lillian brought **me** a book.

The teacher read a story about space travel.
The teacher read **us** a story about space travel.

Yesterday she showed a movie about volcanoes.
Yesterday she showed **the class** a movie about volcanoes.

In the second sentence of each pair, the additional words tell us that the action was directed *toward* someone or something. These words are called **indirect objects**.

> • An **indirect object** is a noun or pronoun that tells *to whom/what* or *for whom/what* an action is done.
> • Indirect objects are used *only* with transitive verbs.
> • If a sentence contains an indirect object, it *must* also contain a direct object.
> • The indirect object always comes *before* the direct object in declarative sentences.

Now look at some more pairs of sentences.

They gave a new bike *to me.*
They gave **me** a new bike.

I bought a new collar *for my dog.*
I bought **my dog** a new collar.

The first sentence in each pair ends with a prepositional phrase that tells *to whom* or *to what* the action of the transitive verb was directed. In the second sentence of each pair, the preposition has been omitted and the noun or pronoun has become an indirect object placed *before* the direct object. These pairs of sentences say the same thing in slightly different ways.

## ■ 8 d Verb Phrases

In Section **4g** you saw that the future tense is created by combining the helping verb *will* with the base form of the main verb.

We *will see* them tomorrow afternoon.

In Section **4j** you saw sentences that combined other helping verbs such as *be* and *have* with main verbs to express actions that are continuing or that have taken place in the past.

We *are working* on the back porch.

I *have waited* two hours for him.

In each example we have combined two verbs to express an action. Whenever two or more related words are used together to create a unit of meaning within the sentence, these words form a *phrase*. In Section **7c** you saw how *prepositional phrases* were used. Now we will look at **verb phrases**.

> - A **verb phrase** contains a *main verb* and one or more *helping verbs*.
> - The **main verb** expresses the most important action in the sentence. It tells exactly what the subject *is* or what it is *doing*.
> - The **helping verb** is another verb that works with the main verb. The helping verb can show that an action will happen in the future. It can also show that an action has been completed in the past or is continuing at the present.

Here are some **declarative sentences** that use verb phrases.

She *is looking* for a scarf to match her coat.

We *are going* to the movie at seven o'clock.

They *have finished* repairing the road.

Each sentence begins with a subject followed by a verb phrase. In each verb phrase, the main verb follows directly after the helping verb. Notice what happens when these same three sentences are changed to become questions.

*Is* she *looking* for a scarf to match her coat?

*Are* we *going* to the movie at seven o'clock?

*Have* they *finished* repairing the road?

The **helping verb** is now placed at the beginning of the sentence *before* the subject, and the **main verb** comes after the subject. This shift in word order allows us to change a *statement* (a declarative sentence) to a *question* (an interrogative sentence).

## ■ 8 e  The Principal Parts of the Verb

You are already familiar with the spelling of regular verbs in the present tense and the past tense.

I *talk* to my grandparents on the phone every Saturday.

My mom *talks* to them, too.

Yesterday we *talked* to them for half an hour.

Here are some more sentences that use other forms of the verb *talk*.

I *am talking* to my friends now.

They *are talking* to the people who live next door.

He *has talked* to everyone who saw the accident.

We *have talked* to them many times.

In each sentence there is a slight difference in the expression of *when* the action of the verb took place. In order to express these differences, we used the four forms that any verb can take. These are called the **principal parts** of the verb.

| Present | Present Participle | Past | Past Participle |
|---------|--------------------|------|-----------------|
| talk | (am) talking | talked | (has) talked |
| look | (is) looking | looked | (had) looked |

- With regular verbs, the present participle adds the inflection *ing* to the base form of the verb.
- With regular verbs, the past participle adds the inflection *ed* to the base form of the verb.

All verb tenses can be formed using these principal parts.

Participles are often used as the **main verb** in the sentence. When they are used this way, they are preceded by **helping verbs**. In the examples above, you saw some of the helping verbs (written in parentheses) that can be used with participles.

**8**

In Sections **8g** and **8h** you will see how the *present participle* is used with helping verbs such as *am*, *is*, *are*, *was*, and *were*. In Sections **8i** and **8j** you will see how the *past participle* is used with the helping verbs *have*, *has*, and *had*.

Here are the principal parts of some regular verbs:

| Present | Present Participle | Past | Past Participle |
|---------|--------------------|------|-----------------|
| blame | blaming | blamed | blamed |
| climb | climbing | climbed | climbed |
| drag | dragging | dragged | dragged |
| extend | extending | extended | extended |
| furnish | furnishing | furnished | furnished |
| grab | grabbing | grabbed | grabbed |
| hope | hoping | hoped | hoped |
| listen | listening | listened | listened |
| locate | locating | located | located |
| pull | pulling | pulled | pulled |
| push | pushing | pushed | pushed |
| refer | referring | referred | referred |
| require | requiring | required | required |
| stop | stopping | stopped | stopped |
| wait | waiting | waited | waited |
| watch | watching | watched | watched |
| wrap | wrapping | wrapped | wrapped |

As always, words that end with a single vowel and a single consonant *double* the final consonant before adding inflections (*stop*, *stopped*, *stopping*). Words that end with *silent e* drop this *e* before adding the inflections *ed* and *ing* (*hope*, *hoped*, *hoping*).

The past tense and the past participle are spelled the same in regular verbs. In Section **8m** you we will see some irregular verbs that have different spellings in the past tense and the past participle.

■  **8 f    Active Voice and Passive Voice**

Before going ahead, we should look at a particular kind of sentence structure which makes use of *verb phrases* involving one of the principal parts discussed above.

Look at the following sentences. They say the same thing, but notice the difference in how they are constructed.

High winds damaged the trees.

The trees were damaged by high winds.

In the first sentence, the emphasis is on the *high winds* and what they *did*: they damaged the trees. In the second sentence, the emphasis is on the *trees* and what was done *to them*: they were damaged by high winds. Both sentences are perfectly good; they just put the emphasis on different words. The first sentence is in the **active voice**, and the second sentence is in the **passive voice**.

---

- When a sentence is in the **active voice**, the subject *performs* the action expressed by the verb.
- In the active voice, verbs often take a direct object.

---

- When a sentence is in the **passive voice**, the subject *receives* the action expressed by the verb.
- Direct objects are not used in the passive voice.

---

You have seen many sentences in the active voice throughout this book. Usually the subject was followed by the verb in the present tense, past tense, or future tense. You have already seen that transitive verbs were followed by direct objects. This is the usual pattern for sentences in the active voice:

**Active Voice**
*The subject **did something** to someone or something.*

Lightning    struck    the tree.

Now look at several sentences in the passive voice. What do you notice about the verbs in each sentence?

This song *is sung* by the tenor soloist.

Seeds *are eaten* by many kinds of animals.

The ball *was hit* by the batter.

These plays *were written* by Shakespeare.

In every sentence a *verb phrase* is used. This phrase always consists of a form of the verb *be* followed by the *past participle* of the main verb. Sentences in the passive voice always use this type of verb phrase.

This is the usual pattern for sentences in the passive voice:

**Passive Voice**
*The subject **has something done to it** by someone/something.*

The tree was struck by lightning.

The passive voice must be handled carefully and should not be used very often. When too many sentences are in the passive voice, the effect can be weak and awkward.

> An exciting game was watched by a very large crowd of fans. The score was very close until the final inning. Then the game was won when a home run was knocked out of the park by the designated hitter, Bubba Smern.

A sportswriter who turned in this account of a close game would probably be told to find another job. Most of the time we want to use the *active voice* for a stronger effect. However, it is sometimes helpful to use the passive voice, especially when you do not know who or what took the action.

> The job was finished before we got there.

> The curtain was closed at the end of the play.

> The game was played by two teams from another town.

Sometimes a sentence can be equally effective in the active voice or the passive voice. You can choose to stress the fact that the subject *does* something (active voice), or you can stress what *was done* to the subject.

> The scientists discovered several dinosaur bones.

> Several dinosaur bones were discovered by the scientists.

# Progressive Forms

## ■ 8 g    The Present Progressive

*Present participles* can be used in a number of ways within the sentence. Often they are combined with helping verbs to form *verb phrases*. In the following sentences you see verb phrases written in boldface.

I **am working** on a project for school.

You **are using** too much paper.

She **is waiting** for the bus.

We **are looking** at some new furniture.

They **are traveling** across the country this week.

These verb phrases are examples of the **present progressive** form of the verb.

> • The **present progressive** is a verb phrase which begins with a form of the helping verb *be* in the *present tense*. This helping verb is followed by the *present participle* of the main verb.
> • The present progressive is used to tell about actions that are continuing at the time they are described.

The following list below shows how the helping verb *be* in the present tense is combined with the present participle of the verb *work* to create the **present progressive** form.

| HELPING VERB + MAIN VERB = PRESENT PROGRESSIVE | | |
| (Present Tense) | (Present Participle) | |
| I am | + working | = I am working |
| you are | + working | = you are working |
| he is | + working | = he is working |
| she is | + working | = she is working |
| it is | + working | = it is working |
| we are | + working | = we are working |
| they are | + working | = they are working |

The present progressive is a verb form we use very often because it tells about actions that continue to take place at the time we are writing or speaking. It can also be used to tell about things we intend to do right away.

I *am studying* for my math test.

She *is reading* a book about dolphins.

We *are planning* to visit my aunt and uncle today.

They *are repairing* the street in front of our house.

## ■ 8 h   The Past Progressive

Look at the following sentences and compare them with the sentences you just saw at the end of Section **8g**:

I *was studying* for my math test.

She *was reading* a book about dolphins.

We *were planning* to visit my aunt and uncle today.

They *were repairing* the street in front of our house.

These sentences tell about things that were going on very recently in the past and may still be going on. The third sentence tells about something that was supposed to have happened, but it may have been delayed for some reason. These sentences use the **past progressive** form of the verb.

- The **past progressive** is a verb phrase which begins with a form of the helping verb *be* in the *past tense*. This helping verb is followed by the *present participle* of the main verb.
- The past progressive is used to tell about actions that began in the past and continued for some time.

The following list shows how the helping verb *be* in the past tense is combined with the present participle of the verb *work* to create the **past progressive** form.

| HELPING VERB | + | MAIN VERB | = | PAST PROGRESSIVE |
|---|---|---|---|---|
| (Past Tense) | | (Present Participle) | | |
| I was | + | working | = | I was working |
| you were | + | working | = | you were working |
| he was | + | working | = | he was working |
| she was | + | working | = | she was working |
| it was | + | working | = | it was working |
| we were | + | working | = | we were working |
| they were | + | working | = | they were working |

The **past tense** tells about actions that have already been completed. The **past progressive** tells about actions that began in the past and continued for some time. You can see the difference in these two sentences:

They **walked** to school yesterday.

They **were walking** to school when I saw them this morning.

# Perfect Tenses

There is another important group of verb phrases we use frequently. These verb phrases make up the **perfect tenses**.

**8**

> • **Perfect tenses** combine a form of the helping verb *have* with the *past participle* of the main verb.
> • The three perfect tenses are the **present perfect**, the **past perfect**, and the **future perfect**.

**Present Perfect:** For the past week we *have learned* about snakes and turtles.

**Past Perfect:** We *had learned* about alligators and crocodiles before we started on snakes and turtles.

**Future Perfect:** By next week we *will have learned* everything there is to know about reptiles.

## ■ 8 i  The Present Perfect Tense

> • In the **present perfect tense**, the helping verb *have* in the present tense is combined with the past participle of the main verb.
> • The present perfect tense is used to express actions which happened at some time in the past or which began in the past and continue in the present.

Here you see the verb *work* in the present perfect tense:

HELPING VERB + MAIN VERB  =  PRESENT PERFECT
(Present            (Past
Tense)              Participle)

| | | | |
|---|---|---|---|
| I have | + worked | = | I have worked |
| you have | + worked | = | you have worked |
| he has | + worked | = | he has worked |
| she has | + worked | = | she has worked |
| it has | + worked | = | it has worked |
| we have | + worked | = | we have worked |
| they have | + worked | = | they have worked |

In the following examples, the first sentence in each pair uses the **past tense** to tell that something has already happened. The second sentence uses the **present perfect** tense to tell us that the same thing has happened a number of times before. Notice that the helping verb is in the present tense (*have* or *has*).

I **raked** the leaves yesterday.
I **have raked** them every Saturday this fall.

They **looked** for four-leaf clovers.
They **have looked** in every yard in the neighborhood.

She **waited** for her friends to arrive yesterday.
She **has waited** all morning for them to arrive.

It **rained** yesterday.
It **has rained** for the past two hours.

## ■ 8 j  The Past Perfect Tense

> • In the **past perfect tense**, the helping verb *have* in the past tense is combined with the past participle of the main verb.
> • The past perfect tense is used to express an action which was completed *before* something else happened.

Here you see the verb *work* in the past perfect tense:

HELPING VERB + MAIN VERB  =  PAST PERFECT
  (Past        (Past
  Tense)      Participle)

| I had | + worked | = | I had worked |
| you had | + worked | = | you had worked |
| he had | + worked | = | he had worked |
| she had | + worked | = | she had worked |
| it had | + worked | = | it had worked |
| we had | + worked | = | we had worked |
| they had | + worked | = | they had worked |

The following sentences use the past perfect tense to make it clear that one action was completed before another took place. Notice that the helping verb is in the past tense (*had*).

We **had finished** dinner before they arrived.

Lions and tigers **had interested** her for several years.

Before he learned more about them, Todd **had believed** that many snakes were poisonous.

After studying for only a few weeks, she **had learned** several new piano pieces.

## ■ 8 k  The Future Perfect Tense

> • In the **future perfect tense**, the helping verbs *will* and *have* are combined with the past participle of the main verb.
> • The future perfect tense is used to express actions which will be completed before some other action takes place in the future.

Here you see the verb *work* in the future perfect tense:

| HELPING VERB<br>*will* | + | HELPING VERB<br>*have* | + | MAIN VERB<br>(Past Participle) | = | FUTURE PERFECT |
|---|---|---|---|---|---|---|
| I will | + | have | + | worked | = | I will have worked |
| you will | + | have | + | worked | = | you will have worked |
| he will | + | have | + | worked | = | he will have worked |
| she will | + | have | + | worked | = | she will have worked |
| it will | + | have | + | worked | = | it will have worked |
| we will | + | have | + | worked | = | we will have worked |
| they will | + | have | + | worked | = | they will have worked |

You can see that the phrase *will have worked* remains the same whether the subject is singular or plural.

Here are a few sentences showing how the **future perfect tense** can be used:

By the time we have finished this project, we **will have learned** a lot about dinosaurs.

By the end of the day we **will have walked** almost twenty miles.

If the team wins today, this pitcher **will have won** eighteen games this season.

# Irregular Verbs

■ 8 1    The Principal Parts of Irregular Verbs: I

You know that some verbs do not simply add **ed** to form the past tense. These **irregular verbs** have different spellings in the present tense and the past tense. We will look at the principal parts of some of the most important irregular verbs.

---

In this group of irregular verbs, the same spelling is used in the **past tense** and the **past participle**.

---

Each verb is first listed in its base form. The participles are listed with the helping verb in the form that would be used in the *third person*.

| Verb | Present Participle | Past | Past Participle |
|------|-------------------|------|-----------------|
| bring | (is) bringing | brought | (has) brought |
| buy | (is) buying | bought | (has) bought |
| catch | (is) catching | caught | (has) caught |
| feel | (is) feeling | felt | (has) felt |
| have | (is) having | had | (has) had |
| leave | (is) leaving | left | (has) left |
| make | (is) making | made | (has) made |
| say | (is) saying | said | (has) said |
| set | (is) setting | set | (has) set |
| sit | (is) sitting | sat | (has) sat |
| teach | (is) teaching | taught | (has) taught |
| think | (is) thinking | thought | (has) thought |

Here are some sentences using forms of the verb *think*:

I **think** about things a lot. (Present Tense)

I **am thinking** about mowing the lawn. (Present Participle)

I **thought** about mowing the lawn yesterday. (Past Tense)

I **have thought** about it enough. (Past Participle)

**8**

### ■ 8 m The Principal Parts of Irregular Verbs: II

We have seen that the spelling of the past participle is sometimes the same as the past tense, even in irregular verbs. In the next list of irregular verbs, you will see that this is no longer the case.

---

In this group of irregular verbs, a different spelling is used in all the principal parts in most instances. A few of these verbs retain the same spelling in the base form and in the past participle.

---

| Verb | Present Participle | Past | Past Participle |
|------|--------------------|------|-----------------|
| be | (is) being | was | (has) been |
| blow | (is) blowing | blew | (has) blown |
| break | (is) breaking | broke | (has) broken |
| choose | (is) choosing | chose | (has) chosen |
| come | (is) coming | came | (has) come |
| do | (is) doing | did | (has) done |
| drink | (is) drinking | drank | (has) drunk |
| eat | (is) eating | ate | (has) eaten |
| fly | (is) flying | flew | (has) flown |
| give | (is) giving | gave | (has) given |
| go | (is) going | went | (has) gone |
| run | (is) running | ran | (has) run |
| see | (is) seeing | saw | (has) seen |
| sing | (is) singing | sang | (has) sung |
| sink | (is) sinking | sank | (has) sunk |
| swim | (is) swimming | swam | (has) swum |
| take | (is) taking | took | (has) taken |
| tear | (is) tearing | tore | (has) torn |
| throw | (is) throwing | threw | (has) thrown |

In the preceding list, notice that the verbs *run* and *come* have the same spelling in the base form and in the past participle (after the helping verb *has*). You can also see that a number of these irregular verbs form the past participle by adding ***en*** to the base word (*eat, eaten; give, given; take, taken*) or to the past tense (*chose, chosen; broke, broken*).

You may not always be sure which form to use for the past tense and the past participle of *sink, drink, swim,* and *sing*. The following sentences show how to use these two parts of speech for each of these four verbs:

A ship **sank** in the storm last week.
Many ships **have sunk** along this coastline in past years.

We **drank** some lemonade yesterday.
Over the past few days we **have drunk** gallons of it.

She **swam** in the relay race yesterday.
She **has swum** for her team in the past five races.

Ann and Susan **sang** with the choir last week.
They **have sung** a number of solos in the past year.

# Other Verb Forms: Verbals

In this section we will look at words called **verbals**.

> - **Verbals** are verb forms that are used as *other* parts of speech, not as verbs.
> - The three major types of verbals are **infinitives**, **participles**, and **gerunds**.

## ■ 8 n    Infinitives

In the following sentences, the main verb is written in italics. Notice the words in boldface.

**To run** in the marathon *was* Ed's greatest wish.

Mai *wanted* **to finish** her homework before dinner.

The words *to run* and *to finish* certainly look like verbs, and they also tell about *doing* something. However, we already have the verbs *was* and *wanted* in these sentences. How are the boldfaced words used?

In the first sentence, the words *to run* function as the *subject*. In the second sentence, the words *to finish* tell what someone wanted to do. These words function as the *direct object* that receives the action of the main verb. The words *to run* and *to finish* are examples of **infinitives**.

> • **Infinitives** are verb forms that can be used as *nouns*.
> • Infinitives usually combine the word *to* with the base form of a verb: *to run, to see, to look*.

Look back at the two sentences about Ed and Mai. What words would you use to answer these questions?

**WHAT** was Ed's greatest wish?

**WHAT** did Mai want?

The first question is answered by the words *to run*, and the second question is answered by the words *to finish*. The answer to each question is a *noun* which names the thing that Ed wished for and the thing that Mai wanted. When we look at these infinitives as words that answer the question WHAT?, we can see that they function as *nouns*.

In the sentences you just saw, each infinitive was followed by a number of other words that formed a *phrase*.

To run in the marathon . . .
. . . to finish her homework before dinner.

> • **Infinitive phrases** contain the infinitive and the other words that are needed to make the meaning complete.

In Chapter 7 you saw that the word *to* is often used as a *preposition*. When it is used this way, *to* is followed by a noun or a pronoun to form a *prepositional phrase*. The preposition *to* was used to relate the noun or pronoun to other words in the sentence.

Do not confuse the use of *to* in prepositional phrases with the use of *to* as part of the infinitive. In the infinitive, *to* is always followed by the base form of a *verb*. The following examples show a *prepositional phrase* in the first sentence and an *infinitive phrase* in the second sentence of each pair.

Please give these books *to Maria*.
She wants **to read** more about early explorers.

We are going *to the grocery store*.
We need **to buy** some grapes and bananas.

Fred and I went *to a baseball game* last Saturday.
We like **to watch** the outfielders catch fly balls.

You will often use an infinitive as the direct object in a sentence. This is the way the infinitive phrases are used in the sentences you just saw. Infinitives often appear in sentences that say "I like" or "I want" or "I need" **to do** something.

## ■ 8o Participles

You have seen that the *present participle* adds **ing** to the base form of a verb. It is often combined with the helping verb *be* to form the *present progressive* and the *past progressive*.

I *am looking* for my socks. (present progressive)

He *was working* in the yard. (past progressive)

The *past participle* usually adds **ed** to the base form of regular verbs. (You saw in Sections **8l** and **8m** that many *irregular verbs* had different forms in the past participle.) The past participle can be combined with the helping verbs *have*, *has*, or *had* to form the *perfect tenses*.

She *has looked* everywhere for her keys.

Her parents *have looked* for them, too.

They *had looked* for an hour before they found them.

Now look at some other sentences that contain the present participle (ending with **ing**) or the past participle (ending with **ed** or **en**). How are these participles used?

*Running* water flowed over the rocks.

*Burned* toast does not taste very good.

Can you repair this *broken* plate?

Here the participles are used as modifiers that tell more about the nouns which follow them: *running water*, *burned toast*, and *broken plate*.

**8**

> • **Participles** can be used as *adjectives*. Both the present participle and the past participle may be used this way.

When a participle is used as an adjective, it is often grouped with other words to form a *phrase*.

> • **Participial phrases** include the participle and all the other words needed to complete its meaning.

In the following sentences the participial phrases are printed in boldface. Each participial phrase modifies the noun that precedes it.

The sunlight **shining on the water** was extremely bright.

The clothes **hanging in the closet** need to be cleaned.

All the books **chosen for this class** are very interesting.

I liked all the presents **given to me**.

### ■ 8 p  Gerunds

There is still another way we can use words that add ***ing*** to the base form of the verb. Look at the following sentences to see what this is.

*Running* is good for you.

*Swimming* is her favorite sport.

I enjoy *hiking* and horseback *riding*.

Each of the italicized words is a **gerund**.

> • **Gerunds** are verb forms that add ***ing*** to the base form of the verb.
> • Gerunds are used as *nouns*.

In the examples you just saw, gerunds were used as subjects in the first two sentences and as direct objects in the last sentence. Each word suggests an action: *running*, *swimming*, *hiking*, and *riding*. By adding the ***ing*** inflection, we are able to express these actions as nouns: things that you can *do*.

Gerunds are often grouped with other words to form phrases.

> • **Gerund phrases** include the gerund and all the other
>   words needed to complete its meaning.

In the following sentences, gerund phrases are printed in boldface.

**Riding a bike** is a lot of fun.

I enjoy **riding my bike** more than anything else.

**Moving all our furniture** was a difficult task.

She spent the last three hours **studying for her test**.

**8**

# *Check Your Understanding*

*Answers begin on p. 287.*

**1. Transitive and Intransitive Verbs**
Underline the verb in each sentence. After each sentence, indicate whether the verb is **transitive** or **intransitive**. (Review Sections **8a** and **8b** if necessary.)

  1.  He plays the piano and the organ.

  2.  This car rides very smoothly.

  3.  We heard the sound of rushing water.

  4.  The car hit a bump in the road.

  5.  She sings very well.

**2.  Direct Objects and Indirect Objects**
The following sentences all contain transitive verbs. Underline the **direct object** once in each sentence. If there is an **indirect object**, underline it twice. (Review Sections **8a** and **8c** if necessary). Here is an example:

  I gave him my apple at lunch.

  1.  We bought two new chairs for the kitchen.

  2.  Mom and dad gave me some money for my birthday.

  3.  I didn't see them at the game.

  4.  We gave her the message you wanted delivered.

  5.  They lost all their suitcases on the trip.

# *Check Your Understanding*

### 3. Principal Parts of Regular Verbs

Here are some verbs in their base forms:

reserve    finish    discard    replace    impress

Write the four principal parts of each verb. In the first column, show not only the base form but also the form that is used in the third person singular in the present tense.

Here is an example showing the principal parts of the verb *push*:

| Present Tense | Present Participle | Past Tense | Past Participle |
|---|---|---|---|
| push, pushes | pushing | pushed | pushed |

### 4. Active Voice and Passive Voice

Look at each sentence and decide whether it is in the active voice or the passive voice. Then rewrite each sentence so that the active voice is changed to the passive voice, and vice versa. Here is an example:

Flames consumed the old barn. (ACTIVE)
The old barn *was consumed* by flames. (PASSIVE)

1. The quarterback completed ten passes.
2. A good time was had by everyone.
3. The band gave a concert last night.
4. The building was shaken by the mild earthquake.
5. His great success surprised everyone.

**8**

# *Check Your Understanding*

### 5. Progressive Verb Forms

The following sentences are all written in the present tense. Rewrite each sentence so that the **present progressive** form of the verb is used. Then write it again with the **past progressive** form of the verb. Here is an example:

> He **works** for his uncle after school.
> He **is working** for his uncle after school.
> He **was working** for his uncle after school.

1. The tree branch **scrapes** against my window.
2. We **rehearse** for the spring program.
3. My brother **competes** in a relay race.
4. All the snow **melts** from the trees.
5. The chipmunk **scurries** across the lawn.

### 6. Perfect Tenses

The following sentences use a verb in the past tense. Rewrite each sentence using the **present perfect** tense. Then write each sentence again using the **past perfect** tense. Review Sections **8i** and **8j** if necessary. You can also review the principal parts of irregular verbs in Sections **8l** and **8m**. Here is an example:

> We **wrote** three letters to them.
> We **have written** three letters to them.
> We **had written** three letters to them.

1. I **carried** all the boxes into the garage.
2. We **watched** for the bus to arrive.
3. My family **went** from Chicago to Cleveland.
4. Ellen **captured** her runaway turtle.
5. The movers **took** all the furniture out of the house.

8

# *Check Your Understanding*

7. **Using Irregular Verbs**

   The following sentences contain verbs in their base forms. Rewrite each sentence, using the same verb in the **past tense**. Review irregular verbs in Sections **8l** and **8m** if necessary.

   1. They **catch** the four o'clock bus yesterday.
   2. The small boat **sink** in the storm
   3. My friends **leave** before I was able to see them again.
   4. He **throw** out a lot of good stuff.
   5. Somebody **drink** all the chocolate milk.

8. **Principal Parts of Irregular Verbs**

   Use the following headings and write the principal parts for each of the irregular verbs listed below. Review Sections **8l** and **8m** if necessary. The verb *choose* is already written in its principal parts.

   | Present | Present Participle | Past | Past Participle |
   |---------|-------------------|------|-----------------|
   | choose | choosing | chose | chosen |
   | do | | | |
   | fly | | | |
   | think | | | |
   | sing | | | |
   | teach | | | |

8

# *Check Your Understanding*

**9. Recognizing Participles and Gerunds**

Underline each participle and each gerund that you find in the following sentences. Draw an arrow from each participle to the word it modifies. At the end of each sentence, indicate whether the underlined word is a participle or a gerund.

Here is an example:

> That was a frustrating experience.
>
> That was a <u>frustrating</u> experience. (Participle)

1. Juggling is his favorite hobby.
2. Their speeding car almost ran off the road.
3. His favorite exercises are jogging and swimming.
4. Our team suffered another humiliating defeat.
5. The crumbling stone wall was more than 100 years old.

**10. Using Participles and Gerunds**

In the following sentences certain words are printed in boldface. Use each word as a participle (adjective) or as a gerund (noun), depending on each situation. At the end of each sentence, indicate whether you have used a participle or a gerund.

Here is an example:

> **Eat** too fast will make you sick.
> **Eating** too fast will make you sick. (Gerund)

1. The **blister** heat made it impossible to keep walking.
2. **Install** the new faucet was not very difficult.
3. That is not a very **convince** argument.
4. **Wander** herds of buffalo roamed the plains.
5. My dog spends most of his time **eat** and **sleep**.

# 9

# More about Sentences

In earlier chapters you saw that *diagrams* can help you to see how sentences are constructed. In this chapter we will use diagrams to review the sentence structures you have already seen. These diagrams will clarify information about parts of speech and about relationships among words in sentences.

Later in this chapter you will look at sentences that are more complicated than the ones you saw earlier. You will also see how to locate errors and how to correct them.

As you look at each diagram, notice that the most important words—the *nouns, pronouns*, and *verbs*—are the ones written on the base line (sometimes called the *main line*). Individual *adjectives* and *adverbs* are written below the word they modify. As we have already mentioned, these parts of speech make up the *vocabulary words* that express much of the meaning of the sentence.

As for the other parts of speech, you will see that *prepositions* are diagrammed to show the relationship between the object of the preposition and the word that is modified by the prepositional phrase. *Conjunctions* are diagrammed to show how they connect one word or part of a sentence to another. These diagrams also show how you can construct sentences by connecting one meaningful *group* of words to another.

## Diagramming Simple Sentences: The Subject and the Predicate

### ■ 9 a    Simple Subjects and Simple Predicates

In Section **1g** you saw that many sentences contain one word that is the most important part of the subject, and in Section **1h** you saw that sentences also contain a verb that is the most important part of the predicate. These words are the *simple subject* and the *simple predicate*. In Section **1i** you saw that the simple subject and simple predicate are written on a *base line* with a vertical line between them:

Now look at the second sentence in the following example:

How did the game turn out? **We lost!**

The second sentence contains *only* a subject and a verb, so it fits the diagram exactly:

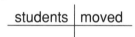

Of course you know that most sentences contain more than two words. For now, we will concentrate on the location of the *subject* and the *verb* on the base line. In the next example you see how these words are diagrammed to show their use in a longer sentence. Later we will see how the other words in the sentence relate to the subject and the verb.

Two students in my class moved to Chicago.

$$\text{students} \mid \text{moved}$$

In an **imperative sentence**, the subject is usually understood and is not written out. In a diagram, the subject can be shown in parentheses in order to make the sentence structure clear:

Close the door.      $\underline{\text{(You)} \mid \text{close}}$

## ■ 9 b   Words That Modify the Subject or the Verb

Whenever there are individual adjectives or adverbs or other words that modify the subject or the verb, these modifiers are written on slanted lines beneath the words they describe. In the next example you see that the possessive pronoun *my* and the adjective *best* modify the subject *friends*, and the adverb *away* modifies the verb *moved*.

My best friend moved away.

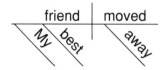

In Section **7e** you saw that *prepositional phrases* could be used as adjectives, and in Section **7f** you saw that they could be used as adverbs. Here is an example to remind you how to diagram a prepositional phrase used as an *adjective*. Notice that the preposition *on* is diagrammed to show how it establishes a relationship between the subject *(people)* and the object of the preposition *(train)*.

The people *on the train* were waving.

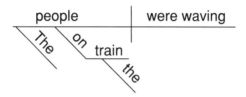

Here is a diagram of a prepositional phrase used as an *adverb* that tells *where* the subject has gone.

They have gone *to the beach*.

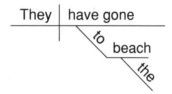

When the sentence contains a *verb phrase* (a helping verb and a main verb), *all* the words in the verb phrase are written on the base line. This shows that the *simple predicate* contains more than one word.

She *is going* to the library.

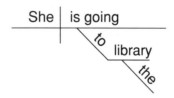

## ■ 9 c   Compound Subjects and Compound Predicates

Some simple sentences contain a **compound subject** which shows that two or more people or things are doing something. The individual words in the compound subject are written on separate lines in a diagram. You will see this in the following example, which also shows the direct object *baseball* written after the verb on the base line. Remember that a short vertical line above the base line is used before a direct object.

**Evan** and **I** | play baseball after school.

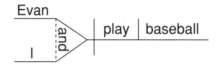

Sentences may also contain a **compound predicate** which tells that the subject is doing two or more different things. The individual words in the compound predicate are also written on separate lines in a diagram. The next example also shows the direct object *grass*, which follows the verb *mowed*, and the direct object *car*, which follows the verb *washed*.

My dad | *mowed* the grass and *washed* the car.

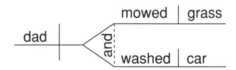

When a simple sentence contains a compound subject *and* a compound predicate, the same procedure is used. The following diagram shows only the words in the subject and the predicate.

My friends and I went to the pool and swam for an hour.

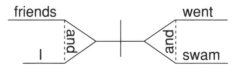

You may wonder how a *simple sentence* can contain a compound subject, a compound predicate, and a number of other modifiers as well.

How can a long sentence like the next one still be considered a *simple* sentence?

> Our visiting relatives and neighbors from Dallas and Fort Worth stayed in several hotels.

The answer is that there is still only *one* subject and *one* predicate in this sentence, even though the subject is compound and there are several words that modify the subject and the predicate. A diagram of the compound subject and the predicate shows that this is a simple sentence.

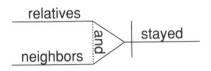

This sentence contains a number of modifiers, especially those made up of *prepositional phrases*. In Section **9b** we reminded you how to diagram prepositional phrases that are used as adjectives or adverbs. Now we will put that information to work to help sort out this sentence.

Look at the sentence again, and then look at a diagram which shows how *all* the other words in the sentence are related to the subject and the verb.

> Our visiting relatives and neighbors from Dallas and Fort Worth stayed in several hotels.

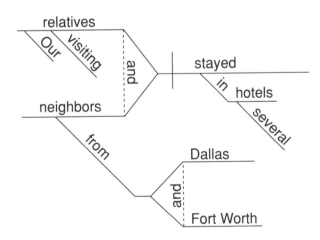

Even though the diagram may look complicated at first, it shows very clearly the compound subject *relatives and neighbors* and the verb *stayed*. It also shows that the prepositional phrase *from Dallas and Fort Worth* serves as an adjective that modifies the subject. The prepositional phrase *in several hotels* serves as an adverb that modifies the verb.

### ■ 9 d    Sentences Containing Participles

Diagrams help you see that words of the same type can be used in different ways. Diagrams also show that sentences which look similar may actually be very different. Notice the words in boldface when you compare these two sentences:

> He **is waiting** in the next room.
> This book **is interesting**.

The first sentence uses the progressive verb form *is waiting*. Here, *is* is the helping verb and *waiting* is the main verb. The prepositional phrase *in the next room* serves as an adverb that tells *where* the subject is waiting.

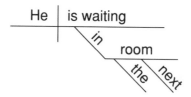

In the sentence "This book is interesting," the words *is interesting* may seem to follow the same pattern, but this sentence is actually very different from the first. Only the word *is* is used as a verb. The word *interesting* is a present participle used as a **predicate adjective** to modify *book*. A diagram will make this clear:

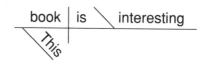

When the *past participle* is used, a diagram can also help to show how the sentence is constructed. Look at these two sentences:

> My uncle has worked on his sailboat for two months.
> He is interested in boats of all kinds.

Both *worked* and *interested* are past participles, and each is preceded by a verb. However, look very closely at *which* verb is used in each sentence. This will help you decide how the past participles are used.

In the first sentence, the main verb *(worked)* is preceded by the helping verb *has*. In Section **8h** you saw that this is a verb phrase which creates the *present perfect tense*. Remember that the perfect tenses always involve the helping verbs *have*, *has*, or *had* followed by the past participle of the main verb.

uncle | has worked

Look at the second sentence again.

He is interested in boats of all kinds.

In this sentence the only verb is the linking verb *is*. The word *interested* is a past participle used as a **predicate adjective** to modify *He* (which refers to *My uncle*).

The word *interested* does not express action and is not part of the verb. Furthermore, *interested* comes after the verb *is*, not *has*, *have*, or *had*. You can tell that *interested* is not used in the past perfect tense because it is preceded by a linking verb, not a helping verb.

# Diagramming Simple Sentences: Complements

You know that sentences contain a subject and a verb, and you also know that many sentences contain a number of other words in the predicate of the sentence. In the examples you have seen on the preceding pages, some sentences contained a *direct object* after the verb and other sentences contained a *predicate adjective*. These additional words are examples of **sentence complements**.

- A **sentence complement** is a word or a group of words that comes after the verb in the *predicate* of the sentence.
- **Object complements** are used after action verbs; they complete the sentence by receiving the action of the verb.
- **Subject complements** are used after linking verbs; they complete the sentence by telling more about the subject.

The word *complement* is a noun derived from the verb *to complete*. The *complement* is the part of the sentence that *completes* the meaning of a sentence. You will find that many sentences follow this pattern:

**Complete Subject** | **Complete Predicate**
(Verb + Complement)

My parents | gave    my brother a new bike.

The subject (*My parents*) and the verb (*gave*) start the process of constructing a sentence, but we need the **complement** to form a sentence that makes sense. In this example the complement contains a *direct object* that tells what was given (*a new bike*) and an *indirect object* that tells who received it (*my brother*).

Diagrams can help you find these three important sentence parts: the subject, the verb, and the sentence complement. In most of the following diagrams we will concentrate on these three elements without always showing all modifiers.

■ **9 e    Object Complements: Direct Objects**

One important sentence complement is the **direct object**. In Section **4c** we pointed out that the direct object is a noun or pronoun that completes the meaning of the sentence by telling *who* or *what* receives the action of a *transitive verb*. Remember that the *direct object* follows the verb on the base line and is preceded by a short vertical line in a diagram.

The first batter hit the ball over the fence.

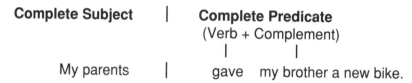

batter | hit | ball

This diagram shows that *ball* is the direct object because it received the action of the verb *hit*.

## ■ 9 f    Object Complements: Indirect Objects

When sentences contain transitive verbs and direct objects, they often contain **indirect objects** as well. The indirect object always comes *before* the direct object and tells *to whom* or *for whom* (or *for what*) an action is done. This indirect object also helps to complete the action of the verb. In a diagram, the *indirect object* is placed below the verb, connected by a slanted line.

Yesterday I gave our dog a good bath.

```
  I | gave | bath
    \dog
```

This diagram shows that *bath* is the direct object; it is the thing that was given. The indirect object *dog* is written below the verb to show that it is the thing *to whom* the bath was given.

## ■ 9 g    Subject Complements: Predicate Nouns and Pronouns

**Subject complements** also appear in the predicate of the sentence, but they follow *linking verbs*, not transitive verbs. Remember that linking verbs such as *am*, *are*, *is*, *was*, and *were* can be used to tell what the subject *is*, not what it *does*.

In Section 4l you saw how predicate nouns and pronouns can be used after linking verbs. In a diagram, the predicate noun is placed on the base line and separated from the verb by a slanted line, not a vertical line.

Carmen is my best **friend**.

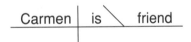

The winner of the first prize was **she**.

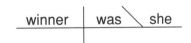

■ **9 h    Subject Complements: Predicate Adjectives**

Many times we have seen predicate adjectives used to describe the subject of a sentence. These adjectives are separated from the word they modify. They often follow verbs such as *is* and *are*, but they may follow other linking verbs such as *seem*, *appear*, and *feel*.

The ancient redwood tree was enormous.

They appeared exhausted after the trip.

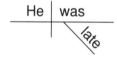

These predicate adjectives modify the subject of each sentence. They tell how the subject *feels* or *looks*, not what it *does*. Each predicate adjective is an example of a *subject complement*.

■ **9 i    Subject Complements: Predicate Adverbs**

Another type of subject complement can be used after linking verbs. These complements are **predicate adverbs** which often tell *where* the subject is or what *condition* it is in. Predicate adverbs are especially helpful in indicating *time* or *place*. As you saw in Section **9b**, adverbs are written on a slanted line below the verb they modify.

He was **late** for dinner.

He | was
late

Those pesky bugs are **everywhere**.

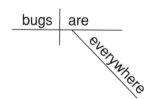

It is important to notice that these predicate adverbs follow *linking verbs*. It is only after linking verbs that a sentence complement can tell more about the *subject*. When complements are used after transitive verbs, they act as objects which receive the action of the verb; they do not tell more about the subject.

# Diagramming Compound Sentences

All the sentences we have seen so far have been *simple sentences*. Each sentence contained *one complete subject* (simple or compound) and *one complete predicate* (simple or compound). Many of the sentences also contained a *complement* which followed the verb in the predicate of the sentence.

Now we will look at diagrams of **compound sentences** which combine two simple sentences. In Sections **1m** and **1n** we talked about compound sentences and pointed out that coordinating conjunctions such as *and* or *but* are used to connect the sentence parts. Diagrams can show very clearly how the two parts of the compound sentence are joined by these conjunctions.

■ **9 j     Compound Sentences Connected by the Word *and***

The next example shows a compound sentence followed by its diagram. Notice how the two parts of the sentence are connected in the diagram.

The weather was good, and the flight was very smooth.

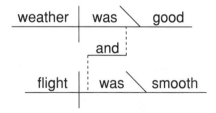

The diagram shows that the first part ("The weather was good") is a simple sentence with its own subject, predicate, and complement. The second part ("the flight was very smooth") is also a simple sentence with its own subject, predicate, and complement. The conjunction *and* is written on a line between the two simple sentences. The vertical dotted lines join the verb of the first sentence to the verb of the second.

### ■ 9 k Compound Sentences Connected by the Word *but*

The next compound sentence shows *contrast* between the two parts.

The rainfall was light, but the wind caused heavy damage.

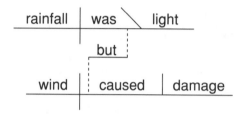

This diagram shows the two simple sentences joined by the conjunction *but*. Here the complement in the first simple sentence is a predicate adjective, *light*; the complement in the second is a direct object, *damage*.

### ■ 9 l Using the Semicolon to Connect Parts of a Compound Sentence

Although the parts of a compound sentence are often joined by *conjunctions*, there is another way of showing how two simple sentences are related. Instead of using a comma at the end of the first simple sentence and beginning the next with a conjunction, you can use the punctuation mark called the **semicolon** (;) between the two parts of the compound sentence.

> He wanted to go to a movie; I wanted to watch TV.
> This book is very interesting; it tells a lot about dinosaurs.

The semicolon *takes the place* of the comma and the conjunction. This punctuation mark shows that the two parts of the compound sentence are of equal importance; they are either very closely *related* or very strongly *contrasted*. When you join the parts of a compound sentence, you may use the semicolon alone or you may use a comma followed by a conjunction. Do not use the comma alone (without a conjunction) between the parts of the compound sentence.

# Clauses and Complex Sentences

In the compound sentences you just saw, each simple sentence was an **independent clause** (also called a *main clause*).

■ **9 m**    **Independent Clauses**

> - A **clause** is a group of words containing its own subject and predicate.
> - An **independent clause** (or **main clause**) makes sense by itself and is able to stand on its own.

You can see that any simple sentence must also be an independent clause.

I like bears a lot.

When you write a compound sentence, you join two independent clauses with a conjunction or with a semicolon. These clauses are of *equal importance*.

I like bears a lot, **but** I wouldn't want to get too close to one.

Now we will look at another kind of clause that is not able to stand on its own.

■ **9 n**    **Dependent Clauses**

In Section **7j** we talked about **subordinating conjunctions** such as *before, after, because, when*, and *while*. These conjunctions were used to introduce groups of words that modified the *independent clause* which was the main part of the sentence.

Be sure to pick up the clothes ***before*** *the store closes*.
We were eager to leave ***after*** *the storm ended*.

The groups of words in italics are called **dependent clauses.**

> • **Dependent clauses** (also called *subordinate clauses*) have their own subject and verb, but they are not complete by themselves. They depend on the rest of the sentence for their meaning.

In order to see the difference between dependent clauses and independent clauses, we can begin with this sentence:

We went to the game, and then we got a pizza.

This is a compound sentence that contains two *independent clauses* which can be written as separate sentences.

We went to the game. Then we got a pizza.

Now look at this sentence, which says the same thing in a slightly different way:

After we went to the game, we got a pizza.

This is *not* a compound sentence. Only the second part of the sentence is an independent clause:

We got a pizza.

Here you see that the two parts of the original sentence are *not* of equal importance. This becomes obvious when you try to use the first part of the sentence by itself:

**After** we went to the game, . . .

Even though the subject is *we* and the verb is *went*, this is not a complete sentence. By beginning with the subordinating conjunction *After*, we have changed the first part of the sentence to a **dependent clause**.

Subordinating conjunctions such as *before, after,* and *because* are often used to introduce dependent clauses, but they are not the only words that can be used for this purpose. It is also possible to use relative pronouns such as *that, who, which,* and *whom* at the beginning of dependent clauses. The word *that* is especially flexible and can be used as a function word in several different situations.

The team **that wins the most games** will get a trophy.
Is this the coat **that he wanted**?
I'm looking for the person **who lost this wallet**.
The man **whom you saw** is my baseball coach.

## ■ 9 o    Complex Sentences

As you have seen, some sentences can contain both dependent and independent clauses. Sentences of this type form a special category called **complex sentences**.

---

- **Complex sentences** contain an *independent clause* and at least one *dependent clause*.
- Whenever a sentence contains a dependent clause, it *must* contain an independent clause as well.
- When the dependent clause begins the sentence, it is often followed by a **comma** before the main clause.
- When the dependent clause comes after the main clause, it is usually not necessary to use a comma.

---

Here are two complex sentences which say the same thing. The first begins with a dependent clause, and the second places the same clause at the end.

**Because the weather was bad**, we decided to postpone our trip.

We decided to postpone our trip **because the weather was bad**.

If the dependent clause at the beginning of the sentence is very short, then the comma may not be needed.

**After Kim left** we went to the mall.

## ■ 9 p    Dependent Clauses Used as Adjectives and Adverbs

In Section **9b** you saw that *prepositional phrases* could be used as adjectives to modify nouns. (Remember that a phrase does *not* contain a subject and verb.) It is also possible to use *dependent clauses* as adjectives to modify a noun. You can see this in the next example:

The cup **that was chipped** is on the table.

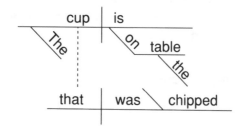

The dependent clause *that was chipped* is written on its own base line below the independent clause. A dotted line connects the dependent clause to *cup*, the word it modifies.

The next example shows a dependent clause that serves as an **adverb** to modify the verb of the sentence:

They gave us some gifts **before we left**.

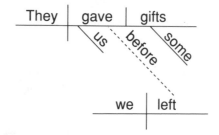

The dependent clause *we left* is written on a base line below the independent clause. The conjunction *before* is written on the dotted line that connects the verb of the independent clause *(gave)* to the verb of the dependent clause *(left)*.

■ **9 q    Phrases, Clauses, and Sentences: A Summary**

At this point it will help to compare the elements of the sentence to see how they work together. Look at these words:

. . . to the movie . . .

This is a prepositional phrase that can be used only as *part* of a sentence. As soon as we add a subject and verb, we can write a complete simple sentence.

**We went** to the movie.

This sentence is an *independent clause*. The phrase *to the movie* serves as an adverb that tells *where* we went.

How can this independent clause be changed to a dependent clause? Just add a *subordinating conjunction* at the beginning:

**Before** we went to the movie, . . .

Now this dependent clause requires something more to complete the meaning and to give us a sentence.

Before we went to the movie, we ate dinner in a restaurant.

The independent second clause now completes the sentence. This example is a *complex sentence* because it contains an independent clause and at least one dependent clause. A diagram shows how all the parts of this sentence fit together.

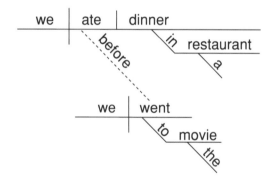

Notice that the dependent clause is placed below the independent clause in the diagram, even though it came at the beginning of the sentence itself.

**9**

# Varying Types of Sentences

## ■ 9 r   Appositives

Look at the pairs of simple sentences given below. A single proper noun (in boldface) is used as the subject in both sentences of each pair. Notice the words printed in italics in the second sentence in each pair.

**Tom** helped us rake the leaves. **Tom** is *my neighbor.*

**Kenya** lies on the Equator. **Kenya** is *a country in Africa.*

**Alaska** is near the Arctic Circle. **Alaska** is *the largest state in the union.*

**George Washington** was from Virginia. **George Washington** was *the first president of the United States.*

In the second sentence in each pair, the words in italics tell us *more* about the word which is also the subject of the first sentence. In fact, we can combine the information in each pair of sentences to form a single sentence.

**Tom**, *my neighbor*, helped us rake the leaves.

**Kenya**, *a country in Africa*, lies on the Equator.

**Alaska**, *the largest state in the union*, is near the Arctic Circle.

**George Washington**, *the first president of the United States*, was from Virginia.

The words in italics are **appositive phrases**. The important word in each phrase is the **appositive**.

> • An **appositive** is a noun or pronoun that follows another noun or pronoun. The appositive tells more about the first noun or pronoun.
> • An appositive is often accompanied by other words that modify it. These words form an **appositive phrase**.

In the examples you just saw, each sentence contained an appositive phrase that modified the subject of the sentence. Notice that the appositive phrase is set off by commas from the rest of the sentence. Now we will look at the subject of each sentence, followed by the noun that forms the **appositive**:

Tom - neighbor          Alaska - state
Kenya - country         George Washington - president

An appositive does not always follow a *proper noun*. Appositives can be used to tell more about *common nouns* as well. In the next sentences, the subject is a common noun (in boldface). The appositive phrase is in italics, and the important noun in the appositive is in boldface italics. The arrows show how the appositive relates to the subject of each sentence.

The **lighthouse**, *a tall stone **building***, looked out over the harbor.

The **infantry**, *well-trained **soldiers** on foot*, advanced through the smoke and noise of battle.

Early **colonists**, ***people** who left Europe to go to the New World*, established Jamestown in 1607.

The old **fortress**, *now only a **ruin***, was built hundreds of years ago.

Here you see the noun that is the subject of each sentence followed by the noun that is the appositive:

lighthouse - building      infantry - soldiers
colonists - people         fortress - ruin

Appositives can be used when you want to give additional information about a noun or pronoun in a sentence. They can help you vary the kinds of sentences you write by showing the close relationship between two pieces of information.

All the appositives we have seen have provided extra information about the *subject*. Often you can use appositives to define terms that might not be familiar to all readers.

**Zeus**, *the most important Greek **god***, ruled from his home on Mount Olympus.

**New Zealand**, *an **island** near Australia*, is in the South Pacific Ocean.

In the sentences we have seen, the appositives were set off by commas to show that they provided information that was extra and was not absolutely vital to the meaning of each sentence. Even if the appositives were omitted, the sentences we have seen would still have made sense.

The **lighthouse** looked out over the harbor.

The **infantry** advanced through the smoke and noise of battle.

Early **colonists** established Jamestown in 1607.

The old **fortress** was built hundreds of years ago.

**Zeus** ruled from his home on Mount Olympus.

**New Zealand** is in the South Pacific Ocean.

In some cases you may want to use appositives that *are* essential to the meaning of the sentence. If you omit these appositives, then the reader may not understand the sentence because important information is missing. In some cases, the sentence may not make any sense at all if the appositive is removed. In sentences of this type, **do not** use commas to set off the appositives. This will let the reader know that the information is very important and is not just added to the sentence.

In the next group of sentences, each appositive is written in boldface. These appositives are not set off by commas because they are absolutely necessary to make the sentence clear.

My sister **Ellen** goes to college.
(This lets you know *which* sister goes to college. Perhaps your sister *Sue* goes to high school.)

The word ***menu*** came into English from French.
(This sentence makes no sense if *menu* is left out. Also, *menu* is written in italics because it is used *as a word*.)

Mark Twain's novel ***Tom Sawyer*** is my favorite.
(You must name the novel if the sentence is to make sense. Titles of books are written in italics.)

> **Appositives** should *not* be set off by commas if the information they provide is essential to the meaning of the sentence.

■  **9 s    Parallel Sentence Structure**

Look at this famous statement by the inventor Thomas Edison:

Genius is one percent inspiration and ninety-nine percent perspiration.

This is effective as much for the *way* it is said as for *what* is said. The reason it is effective is that the subject and verb are followed by two balanced and equally important phrases:

Genius is —⟨ one percent inspiration and
             ninety-nine percent perspiration.

This sentence provides a good example of **parallel structure**.

> When sentences are in **parallel structure**, the parts of the sentence are balanced. The pattern used in the first part of the sentence is followed by the same pattern in other parts of the sentence.

Look at what happens when the parallel structure of Edison's original sentence is canceled out:

Genius is one percent inspiration, and you really have to work hard, too.

What a letdown after such a promising beginning! Now we have only a lame sentence that lacks the impact of Edison's statement.

In Section **71** we looked at *correlative conjunctions*, which are always used in pairs. These conjunctions connect ideas of *equal* importance, and they are often used to create sentences in parallel structure:

**if . . . then**

**both . . . and**

**either . . . or**

**not only . . . but also**

*If* you establish a pattern near the beginning of a sentence, *then* the reader expects to see the pattern completed near the end. For example, if a sentence begins with the word *either*, then the reader expects to find *or* later in the sentence.

**Either** close the window **or** get some more paper towels.

The next sentence tries to point out that someone plays two sports very well. Does this sentence use correlative conjunctions effectively to create parallel structure?

Michael both plays baseball and basketball very well.

This sentence seems to use the correlative conjunctions **both . . . and**, but the word *both* is in the wrong place. Here is the way the sentence should be written:

Michael plays **both** baseball **and** basketball.

A simple illustration will show how these correlative conjunctions work in this sentence:

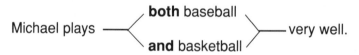

Here we should use the **both . . . and** pattern *after* the verb to show that Michael *plays* both sports very well.

Here is another sentence in which the parallel structure is not clear:

Each student either studied French or Spanish.

Now the conjunction *either* comes before the verb. This suggests that each student *either* **studied** *or* did something else. That is not what the writer means to say. The sentence should show that each student studied one of the two languages.

Each student studied **either** French **or** Spanish.

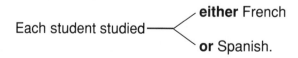

Here is another sentence that does not use correlative conjunctions clearly:

> The students both prepared for their math test and their science projects.

The sentence tries to say that all the students did two things. Here is the way the it should be written:

> The students prepared for **both** their math test **and** their science projects.

> The students prepared for ⟨ **both** their math test
> **and** their science projects.

The following examples are confusing because they do not complete the parallel structure suggested at the beginning of each sentence:

> He **not only** lost his wallet, his coat got torn, too.

> **If** you don't leave early enough, probably you were late to school again.

> **Either** he will get here in time to pick us up, then we were late for the meeting.

Notice that the first part of each sentence establishes one pattern for the subject and verb. It also uses the first part of a correlative conjunction. However, the second part of the sentence does not contain the second part of the correlative conjunction. It also does not balance because it changes the relationship between the subject and verb. Sometimes the verb tenses do not agree, either.

Here is the way these sentences should complete the parallel structure suggested by the correlative conjunctions:

> He **not only** lost his wallet **but also** tore his coat.

> **If** you don't leave early enough, **then** you may be late for school again.

> **Either** he will get here in time to pick us up **or** we will be late for the meeting.

When sentences are in parallel structure, it is especially important for *verbs* agree in tense and number. This is one of the most significant features of parallel sentence structure.

He *waited* for an hour and then *decided* to walk home.

The next sentence is twisted out of shape because verb tenses are mixed: one verb is in the past tense, and the other is in the present tense.

We *went* on vacation and *see* a lot of the country.

If we use both verbs in the past tense, then we can have a well-organized sentence based on parallel structure.

We *went* on vacation and *saw* a lot of the country.

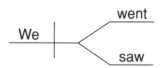

Here is another sentence that contains three elements which *should* follow a parallel pattern, but you can see that one of the elements does not fit:

They like to travel, to ski, and swimming.

The beginning of the sentence sets up a pattern using infinitives (*to travel*, *to ski*), but the pattern is broken by the word *swimming* at the end. In Section **8m** you saw that infinitives contain a verb preceded by the word *to*, and you saw that infinitives are used as nouns. We can maintain the parallel structure by using infinitives consistently:

They like *to travel*, *to ski*, and *to swim*.

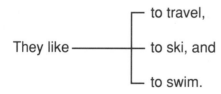

This sentence could also be written another way:

They like *traveling*, *skiing*, and *swimming*.

Now the words that come after the verb are all *gerunds*, verbals ending with *-ing* that are used as nouns.

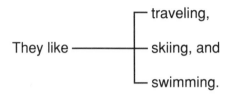

They like
 ┌ traveling,
 ├ skiing, and
 └ swimming.

In both versions of this sentence, we used words *of the same type* in order to follow a consistent pattern. Whenever you set up a particular grammatical structure early in the sentence, then the same structure should be used to present similar ideas. This will allow you to write clear sentences based on the principle of **parallel structure**.

### ■ 9 t    Writing Dialogue: Using Quotation Marks

When students write stories, they sometimes merely give a summary of events: *this* happened and then *that* happened and then *something else* happened. Here is an example:

**Why the Sky Is Blue**
A bear and an ape were talking one night. The bear said that everything in the world should be painted white. The ape said that everything should be painted purple. Mother Nature heard them talking, and she said she didn't want everything painted white or purple. The bear and the ape begged her to think about it, and she said she would. The next day she told the bear to paint one thing white and the ape to paint one thing purple. Then she would paint everything else. The ape said he would paint the sky, but the bear said he wanted to paint the sky. They both threw their white and purple paint into the sky at the same time, and it turned to blue. Even today you can still see blue sky with white patches where the bluish-purple didn't reach.

This just drones on and on, telling what happened but not giving much life to the story. Now look at what a student actually wrote and see how much better it is:

**Why the Sky Is Blue**
One night, when everything was dark, a bear and an ape were arguing. The bear said, "I think everything should be painted white."

**9**

"No! No! Why would you want to do that?" asked the ape. "Everything should be *purple!*"

While this was going on, Mother Nature heard them and didn't like what she heard.

"Not at all! This will not be," said Mother Nature. "That paint would make an awful sight." But the bear and the ape begged and begged, and finally she said she would think about it.

The next day, Mother Nature called the bear and the ape. She said, "I've got an idea! Bear, you may paint one thing white. Ape, you may paint one thing purple. I'll paint the rest of the world."

"OK," the bear and the ape replied.

"I know what I'm going to do," said the ape. "I'm going to paint the *sky!*"

Bear snapped back, "NO! *I'm* going to paint the sky."

And then the bear threw his white paint into the sky just as the ape threw his purple paint. And it made *blue!*

And to this day, you still see blue sky with white where the bluish-purple didn't quite reach.

This version of the story is more interesting because it lets the ape and the bear and Mother Nature do their own talking. Furthermore, it lets us know that the bear and the ape were *arguing*, not just chatting. This story uses **dialogue** to show that the characters are speaking to each other. The word *dialogue* means "a conversation between two or more people." The story also uses exclamations to show that the characters feel very strongly about what they want to do.

Here are some things to remember when you write dialogue:

---

- Each time a person speaks, the words are written within **quotation marks** (" "). These marks are always used in pairs: one quotation mark at the *beginning* of the spoken passage and another at the *end*.
- Whenever one person finishes speaking, the words of the next speaker begin on a new line.
- The spoken passage always begins with a capital letter after the first quotation mark.

  The bear said, "**I** think everything should be painted white."

  "**N**o! No! Why would you want to do that?" asked the ape. "**E**verything should be *purple!*"

---

Notice how we can indicate who is speaking in a dialogue:

---

- A sentence can begin with words such as *he said* or *she said*. When this happens, a comma is placed after the word *said*.

    **She said,** "I've got an idea!"

- Words such as *he said* or *she said* can come at the *end* of the spoken passage. When this happens, a comma is used before the last quotation mark.

    "I know what I'm going to do," **said the ape.** "I'm going to paint the *sky*!"

- If several sentences are spoken by one person, then one set of quotation marks is used for the entire passage.

    The next day, Mother Nature called the bear and the ape. She said, "I've got an idea! Bear, you may paint one thing white. Ape, you may paint one thing purple. I'll paint the rest of the world."

---

Some spoken passages require their own end punctuation, even if the sentence continues beyond the spoken passage.

---

- If the spoken passage asks a question or makes an exclamation, then it ends with its own punctuation mark just before the last quotation mark.

    The ape said, "I'm going to paint the sky!"

- If the sentence continues after the spoken passage, then a period or other end punctuation brings the complete sentence to a close.

    "No! No! Why would you want to do that?" asked the ape.

---

**9**

# Correcting Mistakes in Sentences

Sometimes you may be hurried and may not plan each sentence carefully. You may leave out an important word, or you may break ideas into small bits that don't always make sense. It is also important not to let ideas run on and on without any marks to let the reader know how your thoughts are organized.

On the next few pages you will see sentences written by students your own age. We will look at these sentences in order to see what mistakes there are and how to correct them.

### ■ 9 u  Sentence Fragments

What is not clear in the following sentences?

> This summer my family is going on a trip to Fresno. then to
> Los Angeles.

There seem to be two sentences here, but we can't be sure because the second group of words does not begin with a capital letter. It also does not say *who* is doing something; it makes us look back to see that the writer was talking about *my family* in the first sentence. Furthermore, it does not say *what* is supposed to happen. Again, we have to look back at the first sentence to see that the family is *going on a trip*.

In the example we just looked at, the second group of words is a **sentence fragment**.

> * A **sentence fragment** is only part of a sentence.
>   A fragment is incomplete because it lacks one or more important words.
> * Often the subject or the verb is missing from a fragment.

In the example at the beginning of this section, the fragment did not contain either a subject or a verb. Other sentence fragments may have a subject and verb but may lack a sentence complement. We can correct a sentence fragment by adding the missing words.

> This summer my family is going on a trip to Fresno. **Then we are going** to Los Angeles.

We began the word *Then* with a capital letter to let the reader know that a new sentence is beginning. We also added words to say *who* is going to do something and *what* they are going to do. The word *we* reminds the reader that the subject of these sentences is *my family*. The verb *are going* makes it clear that the family is going on a trip. Now the sentence is complete.

Sometimes we can correct a sentence fragment by using it as part of a **compound sentence**. This is what we have done in the next example.

> This summer my family is going on a trip to Fresno, **and** then **we are going** to Los Angeles.

Instead of writing two simple sentences, we added a comma at the end of the first simple sentence and used the word *and* to connect the remaining words to form a compound sentence. We still need to add the subject and verb *we are going* in order to make the sentence fragment complete.

Here is another example from a student's paper. What simple change would correct the sentence fragment?

> When I grow up, I want to live in a very hot place. Such as California or Florida or any other hot place.

The second "sentence" is really only a phrase that lists examples of hot places. It has no subject or verb. This phrase should be joined to the first sentence to modify the word *place*. All we need to do is remove the first period and the capital letter in the word *Such*:

> When I grow up, I want to live in a very hot place such as California or Florida or any other hot place.

The following sentences are from the same paper.

> I don't like it in Wyoming, because the wind blows to much. But I do like it. Because of the wilderness.

This problem here is similar to the one we saw in the preceding example. The last group of words "Because of the wilderness" is again only a phrase that tells why the writer actually does like Wyoming. Look at the following correction to see how easy it is to fix this error. Did you notice the one misspelled word as well?

> I don't like it in Wyoming because the wind blows **too** much. But I do like it because of the wilderness.

The period before *because* is removed, and the phrase is simply added to complete the preceding sentence "But I do like it." The comma in the first sentence was not needed.

You can check for sentence fragments by always making sure that each of your sentences contains a subject and a verb. (In the imperative sentence, the subject will be understood.) If the subject and verb are clear, then make sure that a sentence complement is provided if it is needed. Then you will have complete sentences, not fragments.

### ■ 9 v    Run-on Sentences

Look at another sentence written by a student your age. Can you see what is not clear in this example?

Swimming is good for your muscles that's why I swim alot.

These words would probably make sense if we heard them spoken. However, when we *read* these words, they are not very clear. This is because there are actually two sentences that have been allowed to run together without any break.

This is the opposite of the example we saw in Section **9u**. Instead of sentence fragments, we now have two sentences that form a **run-on sentence**.

> • **Run-on sentences** result when two or more separate sentences are joined without clear punctuation.
> • The parts of a run-on sentence can be separated and written as individual sentences, or they can be joined by a conjunction to form a compound sentence.

In the example at the beginning of this section, there are no marks to separate the sentences so that the reader can understand them. This problem can be corrected easily.

Swimming is good for your muscles. That's why I swim **a lot**.

The first sentence talked about *swimming* (the subject) and said that it *is good for your muscles* (the predicate). At this point the sentence should end with a period, and a new sentence should begin with a capital letter. The second sentence tells us that the writer likes to swim a lot (remember that *a lot* is written as two words). We already know *why* he or she likes to swim. We have corrected a run-on sentence by dividing it into two separate sentences.

Are these sentences clear to you?

> This summer I'm going to Blue Water Bay. It is supposed to be fun they have swimming pool parties with pizza.

You can see that the second sentence is a run-on sentence. It can also be corrected with a period and a capital letter to divide the run-on sentence into two separate sentences.

> This summer I'm going to Blue Water Bay. It is supposed to be fun. They have swimming pool parties with pizza.

It would not be helpful to combine any of these into compound sentences. We can't really say that one thing happened *and then* another happened.

Here are a two more run-on sentences taken from papers written by students in the middle grades. Look at the changes that are made in the corrected versions.

> There were three strangers coming down the stair, But we reconized them it was our friends in school.
> **There were three strangers coming down the stairs, but we recognized them. They were our friends from school.**

> The zombie ran after her while he was on fire Kathy ran all the way home without looking back.
> **The zombie ran after her while he was on fire. Kathy ran all the way home without looking back.**

Here is one more run-on sentence. How is the correction made in this situation?

> We looked everywhere for the kitten we finally found it under the sink.
> **We looked everywhere for the kitten; we finally found it under the sink.**

In Section **91** we pointed out that the semicolon (;) can be used to take the place of the conjunction in a compound sentence. This is what we have done in this example.

The following run-on sentences tell about things that happened in a logical sequence. How could each of them be corrected?

> The first balloon flight took place in 1782 balloons have been used ever since to carry people aloft.

> The Wright brothers built the first successful airplane they flew it at Kitty Hawk in 1903.

> Others had tried to fly airplanes before no one had succeeded.

> Earlier aviators flew in balloons they flew in gliders that had no engines.

> The design for the helicopter was perfected in 1843 the first successful flight did not take place until 1937.

These would make good *compound sentences* because they contain related bits of information. Notice how the independent clauses are connected in each sentence.

> The first balloon flight took place in 1782, **and** balloons have been used ever since to carry people aloft.

> The Wright brothers built the first successful airplane; they flew it at Kitty Hawk in 1903.

> Others had tried to fly airplanes before, **but** no one had succeeded.

> Earlier aviators flew in balloons, **or** they flew in gliders that had no engines.

> The design for the helicopter was perfected in 1843, **but** the first successful flight did not take place until 1937.

## ■ 9 w  More about Run-on Sentences: Comma Faults

Look at the following sentence and see if there is anything that might be improved:

> Lunch is our free time, we should be able to sit where we want.

This is another kind of run-on sentence. Here we have only a comma between two separate sentences. These would be perfectly good sentences if they were written this way:

> Lunch is our free time. We should be able to sit where we want.

The difference may seem small, but it is important. In the original version, a comma appeared between two sentences. Does the comma *separate* them or *connect* them? Actually, it doesn't do either. This is called a **comma fault** (or a **comma splice**), and it occurs when separate sentences run on with commas thrown in occasionally. These random commas only cause confusion because they avoid a clear connection or a clear separation between sentences.

If you don't believe that these two statements should be connected, then end the first one with a period or other closing punctuation. Begin the next one with a capital letter. This is what we did in the corrected version you just saw.

If you believe that these statements do belong together, then you can *join* them with a *conjunction* after the comma.

Lunch is our free time, **and** we should be able to sit where we want.

In this case you could also use a *semicolon*, which would show how closely related the two ideas are.

Lunch is our free time; we should be able to sit where we want.

Here are a few more run-on sentences containing comma faults. Notice what happens in each corrected version.

Our dog chased a squirrel for five minutes, he didn't catch it.
**Our dog chased a squirrel for five minutes, but he didn't catch it.**

We looked for her dopey mouse all over the place, we finally found it in one of her shoes.
**We looked for her dopey mouse all over the place, and we finally found it in one of her shoes.**

My brother chews gum all the time, I really hate that.
**My brother chews gum all the time. I really *hate* that!**

In these examples you have seen how to correct mistakes. You have also seen how to analyze good sentences in order to discover why they work. Think about some of the things we have talked about in this book: subjects, predicates, and complements; simple, compound, and complex sentences; and so on. The better you understand these elements of sentence structure, the more you increase your ability to write good, clear sentences.

## ■ 9 x   Finding Mistakes

Now we will look at some sentences written by students your age. These sentences contain a variety of mistakes. Some mistakes can be corrected by adding or removing punctuation marks, and other sentences have problems with verb tenses.

In the following examples, errors and their corrections are marked in boldface. After each example you see an explanation of what was changed.

> The other teammates on the other **team, towered** high above me.
> The members of the other **team towered** high above me.

(The comma is not needed because the first part of the sentence is the complete subject. It should move directly to the verb *towered* without any further punctuation. We also don't need to use *other* so many times.)

> A few hours later they **got** something to eat and **walk** around for a while in the shops and in the game room.
> A few hours later they **got** something to eat and **walked** around for a while in the shops and in the game room.

(The first part of the sentence uses the verb *got* in the past tense. The next verb should also be in the past tense to be consistent.)

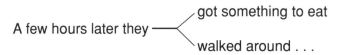

> As morning arrived the sun was like a flashlight **shining** right into her eyes and **blinded** for a moment.
> As morning arrived, the sun was like a flashlight **shining** right into her eyes and **blinding her** for a moment.

(The words *shining right into her eyes* describe the flashlight. The word *blinding* should be used to match *shining*, and the word *her* should be used to show *who* was blinded. The following illustration shows how these changes clarify the *parallel structure* of this part of the sentence.)

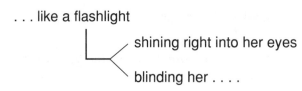

Here is another way the sentence could be clarified:

As morning arrived, the sun was like a flashlight **shining** right into her eyes. **It blinded her** for a moment.

(Now we have written two separate sentences. The second sentence begins with *it*, which refers to the shining sunlight, and the words *blinded her* tell what the light did.)

The next example is taken from a composition written by a student your age. Can you tell why most of the sentences are very good? Can you find the sentence that is not completely clear?

My heroine is ___. She has a great personality and gets me out of jams.
She likes her job and is good at it. One day after work when I did not have a ride home from soccer practice she came and got me and brought me home.
When she wakes up in the morning she gets ready for work feeds her dogs goes to work comes home and spends time with her husband.

Some of these sentences show how to use *compound predicates*. The subject is clearly established first, and then the sentence tells that the subject did two or more things. For example, this is the second sentence in the first paragraph:

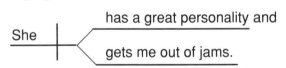

Another kind of sentence is found in the second paragraph. This sentence is very long, but it is also very well written:

One day after work when I did not have a ride home from soccer practice she came and got me and brought me home.

This is a *complex sentence*. It begins with a long *dependent clause* and ends with an *independent clause*. Look first at the independent clause, which tells what happened:

. . . she came and got me and brought me home.

This has a single subject (*she*) followed by three verbs: *came, got,* and *brought*. All the verbs are in the past tense, as they should be. Now you can see that the first part of the sentence tells when these things happened: "One day after work when I did not have a ride home from soccer practice."

Only the final sentence needs a little repair work:

> When she wakes up in the morning she gets ready for work feeds her dogs goes to work comes home and spends time with her husband.

It's difficult to keep track of things in this sentence. The writer may have been rushed and may have forgotten to use enough punctuation. We don't have to change any words, but some commas would help to clarify the *sequence* of phrases:

> When she wakes up in the morning she gets ready for work, feeds her dogs, goes to work, comes home, and  spends time with her husband.

Can you see that this sentence uses ideas we have already talked about in the earlier sentences in this composition? First of all, it is a *complex sentence.* The dependent clause comes at the beginning:

> When she wakes up in the morning . . .

The subject of this clause is *she* and the verb is *wakes up.* The conjunction *when* lets you know that this clause is going to be used as an adverb to tell the *time* of the action of the verbs in the independent clause.

Now look at the final independent clause. This is full of verbs, and all the verbs are correct. This clause forms a simple sentence with one subject (*she*) and five verbs: truly a *compound predicate.* This simplified illustration shows how the sentence fans out into the compound predicate at the end:

In the next example you see the beginning of a story written by a student in the middle grades. You should be able to spot any misspelled words right away. Are there other mistakes that need to be corrected?

### The Great Battle
> A long, long time ago back when there were wizard's, knights, warriors, and of corse king's. There was a story told

> about one king and one knight and a very special sword. This sword had a name and its name was Excalibur, The Kings name was Author and the knight was Lancelot. One day will riding though his country Author Heard a very unuasually load roar of lightnig but it was'nt lightning it was Excaluburs blade crashing through stone Author then found Excalibur & then he seen Lancelot in a distance over a old mossy creaky bridge between two mountians.

We can look at each sentence to see what corrections may be needed. (Individual words that contain mistakes are written in **boldface**. These mistakes will be corrected later.)

> A long, long time ago back when there were **wizard's**, knights, warriors, and of **corse king's**.

You know that the apostrophe is not used to write the plural form of nouns, and you can also see that the word *corse* is misspelled. Aside from these mistakes, can you see any other problems? Is this even a sentence? It tells that there were wizards, knights, warriors, and kings a long time ago, but what did they *do*? Actually this is only the beginning of a longer sentence. If we add the second sentence to the first, then things begin to make sense. (All corrections are written in ***boldface italics***.)

> A long, long time ago, back when there were ***wizards***, knights, warriors, and (of ***course***) ***kings***, there was a story told about one king and one knight and a very special sword.

Now look at the next sentence in the story:

> This sword had a name and its name was Excalibur, The **Kings** name was **Author** and the knight was Lancelot.

This should be written as two separate sentences, and it would also help to use commas to make each sentence clear:

> This sword had a name, and its name was Excalibur. The ***king's*** name was ***Arthur***, and the knight was Lancelot.

Look again at the last part of the example as it was originally written:

> One day **will** riding though his country **Author** Heard a very **unuasually** load roar of **lightnig** but it **was'nt** lightning it was **Excaluburs** blade crashing through stone **Author** then found

**9**

Excalibur **&** then he **seen** Lancelot in a distance over **a** old mossy creaky bridge between two **mountians**.

This long run-on sentence can be rewritten as several shorter sentences. Look at the following version and find all the changes that have been made:

One day *while* riding through his country *Arthur* heard an *unusually* loud roar of *lightning*. But it *wasn't* lightning; it was *Excalibur's* blade crashing through stone. *Arthur* found Excalibur, *and* then he *saw* Lancelot in the distance over *an* old, mossy, creaky bridge between two *mountains*.

Misspellings have been corrected, and punctuation has been added to form three complete sentences. Notice especially the commas used to separate the adjectives *old, mossy, creaky bridge* in the last sentence.

As we corrected this example, we used a number of the principles we have talked about in this chapter. The most important thing is to realize that the original run-on sentence needs to broken into shorter sentences that are clear and complete in their own right.

**9**

# *Check Your Understanding*

## Diagramming Simple Sentences
*Answers begin on p. 292.*

Make a diagram for each of the sentences given below. In the diagram, show only the subject, the verb, and the sentence complement on the base line. Do not diagram other words in the sentences. All sentence complements will be direct objects, predicate nouns, or predicate adjectives. Review Sections **9e, 9g,** and **9h** if necessary. Here is an example:

The movie was extremely boring.

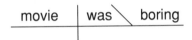

1. We moved the table into the garage.

2. Mr. Edwards is the mayor of our town.

3. They cleared all the trash out of the alley.

4. This book is extremely interesting.

# *Check Your Understanding*

## Diagramming Compound Sentences

Make a diagram of each of the compound sentences given below. Show only the subject, the verb, and the sentence complement on the base line for each part of the sentence. Review Sections **9j** and **9k** if necessary. Here is an example:

The game was unusually long, but it was very exciting.

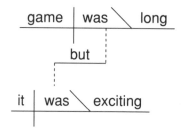

1. The trip was fun, and we visited many places.

2. The outfielder caught the ball, but the runner scored a run anyway.

3. Mrs. Gomez is my teacher, and she is also our basketball coach.

4. The test was difficult, but I got a good grade.

# *Check Your Understanding*

## Clauses and Complex Sentences

Look at each of the following complex sentences. First write the **independent clause** from each sentence. Then write the **dependent clause** below the independent clause. Label each one. Review Sections **9m** through **9q** if necessary. Here is an example:

> Before we left, we made sure the windows were locked.
>
> **Independent:** we made sure the windows were locked.
> **Dependent:** Before we left,

1. They stopped for pizza after the game ended.

2. When we went on vacation, we traveled through four states in one day.

3. He finished the puzzle before I knew what had happened.

4. After the storm ended, the streets were flooded.


## Appositives

Each pair of short sentences can be written as a single sentence using an **appositive**. Rewrite each pair of sentences, using the words in italics as the appositive. Here is an example:

> Evan plays first base. Evan is *the captain of the team.*
> Evan, the captain of the team, plays first base.

1. Tom's dad let us see inside a plane. Tom's dad is *an airline pilot.*

2. The giraffe eats leaves from the tops of trees. The giraffe is *a long-necked animal.*

3. My horse has a long mane and tail. My horse is *a palomino named Beauty.*

4. My friend helped me when I needed it most. My friend is *Karen.*

**9**

# *Check Your Understanding*

## Correcting Mistakes in Sentences

1.  These examples are either run-on sentences or sentence fragments. Rewrite each example so that there are two **simple sentences**. Add any words needed to complete the fragments, and separate the run-on sentences.

    1.  First we flew to Chicago then we drove to Milwaukee.

    2.  We asked for directions they told us which way to go.

    3.  They played baseball for a while. then football.

    4.  The first show was good I didn't like the other one.

    5.  John finished his homework. went to see his friend.

2.  Here are some run-on sentences. Correct each one by changing it to a **compound sentence**. Add a comma and use *and* or *but* when you write each new compound sentence on your paper. Here is an example:

    > I thought we would win the game we didn't.
    > I thought we would win the game, **but** we didn't.

    1.  John watched the movie for a while he didn't like it.

    2.  They waited for a while then they left.

    3.  I saw him across the street he didn't see me.

    4.  Evan watched the game Roy watched it, too.

    5.  Bill and I went to the zoo we saw a lot of animals.

# *Check Your Understanding*

**Correcting Mistakes in Sentences** (continued)

**3.** These examples contain sentence fragments along with complete sentences. In each example, combine the sentence and the fragment into a **compound sentence**. Add some words to the fragments whenever necessary. Here is an example:

> We waited for them to change clothes. then left.
> We waited for them to change clothes, **and** then **we** left.

1. Bill tried very hard. but didn't win.

2. We asked them to go. they didn't want to.

3. My friends met me after school. went to play ball.

4. We left an hour early. still didn't get there on time.

5. There was a boy named Tom. wanted to play football.

# 10

# Word Study

In the English language, many words are very short and are complete all by themselves: *rain, house, dog, light*. However, many other words are longer and are made up of two or more individual parts: *anyone, sidewalk, reopen, education*. The better you understand how words are constructed, the better you will understand what they mean and how to spell them.

## ■ 10a    Base Words and Word Roots

Throughout this book we have talked about *base words*.

> - **Base words** are complete words that make sense by themselves. The base form gives the primary meaning of the word in the English language: *sky, run, rabbit, wander*.
> - Other word parts can be added to change the form of the base word or to create new words.

For example, many base words are singular nouns. Most of these can be changed to the plural by adding an inflection, usually *s* or *es*.

    book, books    glass, glasses

Many other base words are verbs that can be changed from present tense to past tense by adding an inflection, usually *ed*.

    look, looked    mix, mixed

In addition to base words, there are other important word elements called **roots**.

> - **Roots** are word parts that have been taken into English from other languages.
> - Roots give part of the meaning of a word, but they are not complete words in their own right. Roots *must* be combined with other word parts to form complete words in English.

The roots of many English words can be found in *Latin*, a language spoken centuries ago. The list below gives a few English words built on roots taken from Latin. Following each English word you see the root and the Latin word from which it comes.

| ENGLISH WORD | ROOT from LATIN WORD |
| --- | --- |
| ed**uc**ate | *duc-* from *ducere*, to lead |
| e**vid**ent | *vid-* from *videre*, to see |
| **fac**tory | *fac-* from *facere*, to do or make |
| **sci**ence | *sci-* from *scire*, to know |
| trans**fer** | *fer-* from *ferre*, to carry |

English is filled with words and word parts borrowed from Latin and from other languages as well. This often explains why the spellings of some English words may be difficult. Over the centuries, pronunciation has changed while spelling has retained letters that indicated how words were written and pronounced in their original language.

On the following pages we will often use the word *syllable*. Before we go on, you should be clear about the meaning of this important word.

---

### SYLLABLES

A syllable is a word part that can be pronounced as a single sound.

Short words often contain only one syllable: *at, it, up, no, itch; cat, fit, cup, not, pitch.* As you see, each syllable contains a vowel along with consonants after the vowel and sometimes before it as well.

Some other one-syllable words contain two vowels that blend together to form one sound: *boy, out, spoil, sprout.* Many one-syllable words have several consonants before or after the vowel: *chase, float, stretch.*

Most words have more than one syllable. Sometimes, one of the syllables contains only a vowel: *o-pen, a-gain.* More often, there are consonants before or after each vowel: *ba-by, fran-tic, sym-bol, sep-a-rate, di-no-saur, an-tic-i-pate.*

---

Now you will see how to use special kinds of syllables that combine with base words and word roots to form new words.

■ **10 b    Affixes**

Each of the following base words or roots has been changed by the addition of other syllables at the beginning or end. These added syllables are called **affixes**:

read, **re**read, read**er**
act, act**ive**, act**or**
luck, luck**y**, **un**lucky
(*duc-*) **pro**duc**er**
(*spec-*) **re**spect**able**

> • An **affix** is a syllable added to the beginning or the end of a base word or root. Affixes are not words in their own right, but they can affect the meaning of the base word. They can also help to form new words that may be used in ways different from the original word.
> • There are two types of affixes: **prefixes** and **suffixes**.

■ **10 c    Prefixes**

Here are a few familiar words:

lock            correct
agree          build

Notice what happens when we make the following changes:

**un**lock        **in**correct
**dis**agree      **re**build

These words have been changed by the addition of other word parts called **prefixes**.

> • A **prefix** is an affix placed *in front of* a base word or a root. Prefixes are syllables such as *un-*, *in-*, *re-*, or *dis-*. They do not stand on their own, but they are important because they affect the word that follows.
> • Prefixes change the *meaning* of the word to which they are added, but they do not alter the *spelling* of that word.

## ▮ 10 c.1  *un-, mis-, dis-, non-*

These are called **negative prefixes** because they mean "not." These prefixes cause a word to have the *opposite* of its original meaning. Notice that some of these words are verbs, some are adjectives, and a few are nouns.

| | |
|---|---|
| unhappy | unable |
| uncovered | uncomfortable |
| unlucky | unknown |
| unbelievable | unconscious |
| | |
| mismatched | misunderstand |
| misquoted | misjudge |
| mislead | misgivings |
| misfortune | misbehave |
| | |
| disloyal | nonstop |
| dishonest | nonprofit |
| disorganized | nonfiction |
| disqualify | nonviolent |

## ▮ 10 c.2  *in-, im-, il-, ir-*

Another group of prefixes also means "not" or "without." The basic prefix in this group is *in-*, which can be used before words beginning with a number of different consonants and vowels.

correct, incorrect          formal, informal
visible, invisible          accurate, inaccurate
definite, indefinite        expensive, inexpensive
active, inactive            effective, ineffective

---

## ABSORBED PREFIXES

When the prefix *in-* is used before words or roots beginning with certain letters, the prefix is *absorbed* by the following word. This means that the last letter of the prefix is changed to agree with the first letter of the following word or root. This change makes pronunciation much easier and clearer. (*Absorbed prefixes* are also called *assimilated prefixes*.)

---

For example, the prefix *in-* changes to *im-* when it is used before words beginning with *m* or *p*.

mature, immature            patient, impatient
movable, immovable          perfect, imperfect
modest, immodest            polite, impolite
mortal, immortal            possible, impossible

The prefix *in-* changes to *il-* before words beginning with *l*, and it changes to *ir-* before words beginning with *r*.

legal, illegal              relevant, irrelevant
legible, illegible          responsible, irresponsible
literate, illiterate        reversible, irreversible
logical, illogical          resistible, irresistible

Remember that prefixes do not alter the spelling of the following word. This means that words beginning with *il-* will be followed by another *l* in the beginning of the base word or root itself. Words beginning with *ir-* will be followed by another *r* in the beginning of the base word or root. If you remember this, it will help you avoid misspellings such as *ilegal* or *irelevant*.

■ **10 c.3    *com-, col-, con-***

Many Latin words began with the prefix *com-*, which means "with" or "together" in that language. English has borrowed some of these words from Latin, and many of them suggest the idea of doing something *with* someone or something else. Listed below are some English words that begin with the prefix *com-*. Notice that this prefix is used before the letters *b*, *m*, and *p*.

| | |
|---|---|
| combat | compact |
| combine | companion |
| command | company |
| committee | complete |
| communicate | compare |
| comment | computer |

When the prefix *com-* is used before words or roots beginning with other consonants, it is also *absorbed* by the following root.

For example, when *com-* is used before roots beginning with *l*, the spelling of the prefix changes to *col-*.

| | |
|---|---|
| collapse | college |
| collect | collide |
| collaborate | colleague |

The spelling of this prefix changes to *con-* before words beginning with all other letters.

| | |
|---|---|
| connect | consider |
| concentrate | construct |
| condemn | continue |
| conduct | congratulate |

Some of these words still suggest the idea of doing something *with* somebody or something else (*colleague, committee, connect, communicate*). However, you should not always expect to see the literal meaning of the word *with* in every one of the words listed above. Some words have changed their meaning in the many centuries since English began to be influenced by Latin. The important thing is to see how the English word is *constructed* from the Latin prefix and the following root, which is often Latin as well.

### ■ 10 c.4 *ad-, ac-, af-, ap-, as-, at-*

The Latin prefix *ad-* originally meant "to" or "at" or "toward." This prefix was also used in many Latin words that have been taken into the English language. In some words, the meaning "to" or "at" is still obvious.

In other words, the meaning has changed over time, but the spellings have remained.

The following list gives some English words beginning with *ad-*. The original Latin word and its meaning are also given.

ENGLISH    LATIN

addition    *additio*, from *addere* (to add)
adhere      *adhaerere* (to stick to something)
adjacent    *adjacere* (to lie next to something)
admire      *admirari* (to wonder; to marvel at something)

The prefix *ad-* is also *absorbed* when it is used before roots beginning with other consonants.

For example, this prefix changes to *ac-* when it is used before Latin words or roots beginning with *c* and *q*. In English the same principle is applied to the word *acknowledge*.

ENGLISH    LATIN

accept        *acceptare* (to receive)
accident      *accidere* (to fall down)
acclaim       *acclamare* (to shout, cry out)
accommodate *accommodare* (to make fit)
acquaint      *accognoscere* (to know perfectly)
acquire       *acquirere* (to seek, obtain)

When it is used before words beginning with *f*, the prefix *ad-* changes to *af-*.

ENGLISH    LATIN

affect      *affectare* (to influence)
affirm      *affirmare* (to make firm)
affix       *affigere* (to fasten to)
afflict     *affligere* (to strike, cast down)

In the following words you can see that this prefix changes to *ap-*, *as-*, or *at-* to conform to the first letter of the following Latin root.

**10**

| ENGLISH | LATIN |
|---------|-------|
| appear | *apparere* (to become visible) |
| apply | *applicare* (to fold) |
| approve | *approbare* (to approve of) |
| assign | *assignare* (to mark) |
| assist | *assistere* (to cause something to stand) |
| assume | *assumere* (to take) |
| attempt | *attemptare* (to touch, try) |
| attend | *attendere* (to stretch to) |
| attract | *attrahere* (to draw to, pull toward) |

If you remember that *ad-* and its other forms are **prefixes**, then you will be more likely to remember that the consonant at the end of the prefix is usually doubled because the following root starts with the same letter. This can help you remember how to spell words such as *accommodate*, *afford*, *approve*, and *attract*.

### ▌ 10c.5   *de-, dis-, un-*

The prefixes **de-**, **dis-**, and **un-** can be used when we want to *reverse* the action of a verb or indicate that something is *removed*.

| | | | |
|---|---|---|---|
| decode | disagree | unlock | unpack |
| defuse | disobey | untie | unwrap |
| depopulate | displease | unload | unbutton |
| decontrol | disconnect | uncover | unfasten |

In Section **10c.1** you saw the prefix *un-* used before adjectives (*unhappy*, *unlucky*). Here this prefix is used before verbs to show that an action is undone or reversed.

### ▌ 10c.6   *pre-, fore-, post-, re-*

The prefixes **pre-** and **fore-** mean "before."
The prefix **post-** means "after."

| | | |
|---|---|---|
| precook | foresee | postwar |
| preheat | forecast | postpone |
| prefix | foreclose | postscript |
| prehistoric | forehead | postdate |

The prefix *re-* often means "again."

| | |
|---|---|
| reread | reopen |
| rewrite | recycle |
| restart | recapture |
| reelect | reconstruct |

This prefix can also mean "back."

| | |
|---|---|
| return | regain |
| recall | retrieve |
| remember | restore |
| recover | repel |

## ■ 10 c.7 *pro-, super-, sub-*

The Latin word *pro* means "forward" or "before" or "in front of." As a prefix, it suggests the idea of moving forward.

| | |
|---|---|
| proceed | project |
| proclaim | promote |
| produce | propel |
| progress | propose |

The Latin word *super* means "over" or "above." It is used as a prefix in words that suggest the idea of doing something to a greater extent than normal ("*Superman* had *superhuman* strength").

| | |
|---|---|
| supersonic | supercool |
| supercharge | superheat |
| superior | superlative |
| supervise | supernatural |

The Latin word *sub* means "under" or "below." When it is used as a prefix, its spelling changes to *sup-* with word roots that begin with *p*.

| | |
|---|---|
| subject | supply |
| submarine | support |
| subdivide | supplement |
| submerge | suppose |

■ **10 c.8**  *ex-, in-, inter-, extra-*

The Latin word *ex* means "from" or "out of." It is often used as a prefix in words that suggest moving away from something.

| | | |
|---|---|---|
| exit | expel | express |
| export | expand | exhaust |
| exceed | excavate | |

The Latin word *in* means "in" or "into." It is often used as a prefix in words that suggest moving into something or joining one thing to another.

| | | |
|---|---|---|
| include | induct | involve |
| insert | increase | incline |

*In-* changes to *im-* before words beginning with *m* or *p*.

| | |
|---|---|
| immerse | implicate |
| implant | import |

Earlier you saw the word *export*, and here you see the word *import*. Because the root *port-* is from the Latin *portare* (to carry), these words clearly mean "to carry something out or away" (*export*) and "to carry something in" (*import*).

The Latin verb *migrare* means "to remove from one place to another." From this verb we have the word *migrant*: someone who moves from one place to another. The prefixes *ex-* and *im-* can be used to indicate the direction in which someone moves.

emigrant: someone who moves *away from* a country.

immigrant: someone who moves *into* a country.

Notice that the spelling of *ex-* changes to *e-* in order to fit the consonant at the beginning of *migrant*.

The Latin word *inter* means "between" or "among." It can be used as a prefix in words that suggest the idea of moving between two things.

| | | |
|---|---|---|
| interstate | international | interface |
| intercept | intermediate | interval |
| interchange | intercontinental | |

The Latin word *extra* means "outside" or "beyond." It can be used as a prefix in words that suggest *moving beyond* or doing something *in addition to* something else.

> extract
> extravagant
> extraordinary
> extraterrestrial ("Out of this world - ET")
> extrovert (notice the change in spelling to *extro-*)

### ■ 10 c.9 *uni-, bi-, tri-, quart-, dec-, cent-, semi-*

Look at the following prefixes. Each is derived from a Latin or Greek word spoken more than 2,000 years ago. After each prefix you will see the original word and its meaning.

> *uni-* from Latin *unum* (one)
> *bi-* from Latin *bis* (twice)
> *tri-* from Latin *tres* (three)
> *quart-* from Latin *quartus* (fourth)
> *dec-* from Greek *deka* (ten)
> *cent-* from Latin *centum* (hundred)
> *semi-* from Latin *semi-* and Greek *hemi-* (half)

You can see how these prefixes are used to specify *number* in the following words.

> unit - *one* thing that is part of a larger group
> unite - to join several things into *one* thing
> union - a thing formed by joining several things into *one*
> unicycle - a vehicle with *one* wheel
>
> bicycle - a vehicle with *two* wheels
> biannual - happening *twice* a year
> binary - consisting of *two* parts
> bilingual - able to speak *two* languages
> bimonthly - happening every *two* months
> binocular - using *both* eyes
>
> triangle - a figure with *three* angles
> tricycle - a vehicle with *three* wheels
> triple - containing *three* parts
> triplets - groups of *three*

trio - a group of *three*
triceratops - a dinosaur with *three* horns

quart - *one fourth* of a gallon
quartet - a group of *four* people or things
quarter - *one fourth* of something
quarterly - happening *four* times a year

decade - a period of *ten* years
decagon - a figure with *ten* sides
decathlon - athletic contest consisting of *ten* events

century - *one hundred* years
cent - *one hundredth* of a dollar
centigrade - relating to the temperature scale that runs from zero
      (freezing) to *one hundred* (boiling)
centimeter - *one hundredth* of a meter
centipede - a small worm with many legs (*centipede* literally
      means "one hundred feet")

The prefix *semi-* can mean "half"; it can also mean "partly" or "happening twice within a time period."

semicircle - *half* a circle
semiannual - happening *twice* a year
semimonthly - happening *twice* a month
semiweekly - happening *twice* a week
semiprofessional - working part time at a paying job or sport.
semiprecious - having some worth, but not of the highest value
(often refers to gems and minerals such as
amethysts, which are less valuable than diamonds).

### ■ 10d    Suffixes

Here are some familiar words:

luck         enjoy
swim        connect

What happens when affixes are added to the end of each word?

luck**y**       enjoy**ment**
help**er**      connect**ion**

These added word parts (in boldface) are called **suffixes**.

---

- A **suffix** is a syllable placed at the *end* of a base word, a root, or another suffix.
- Suffixes usually do not change the basic meaning of a word, but they often do change a word from one part of speech to another.
- Sometimes the spelling of the base word must be changed when suffixes are added.

---

Suffixes are often used to derive a new word with a meaning that is related to the original meaning of the base word or root. For example, you can see how the word *govern* changes its part of speech in the following sentences. However, each derived word still relates to the original meaning of the word *govern*.

Elected officials *govern* the country and each state.

The *govern**or*** is the most important elected official in the state.

The state *govern**ment*** is situated in the capital city.

The verb *govern* in the first sentence tells what elected officials do. In the second sentence, the noun *governor* names the person who governs. The noun *government* in the last sentence names the organization that governs, or it refers to the process of governing. The two nouns are formed by adding the suffixes -***or*** and -***ment*** to the verb *govern*.

These suffixes were added without changing the spelling of the base word. However, you will encounter suffixes that do require some change in the base word (or root) when they are added. In the following sections, these changes will be discussed whenever they apply.

In Section **6a** you saw that the suffix -*ly* is most often used to derive *adverbs* from other words, especially adjectives. In the following sections you will see suffixes that are used to form other parts of speech.

## ■ 10e    Noun-Forming Suffixes

Many verbs can be changed to nouns by adding certain suffixes. You already saw this in the verb *govern* and the nouns *governor* and *govern-ment* in Section **10d**.

**10**

### ■ 10 e.1    *-er* and *-or*

The suffixes *-er* and *-or* are often used to change *verbs* to *nouns*. When these suffixes are added to verbs, they name the person or the thing that performs the action of the verb.

| | |
|---|---|
| teach, teacher | act, actor |
| jog, jogger | sail, sailor |
| swim, swimmer | instruct, instructor |
| pitch, pitcher | survive, survivor |
| consume, consumer | supervise, supervisor |
| produce, producer | invent, inventor |

Notice that the final *e* in words such as *consume* and *survive* is dropped before these suffixes are added. Whenever a base word ends with a vowel (especially silent *e*) and the suffix also begins with a vowel, the vowel at the end of the base word is usually dropped.

The suffixes *-er* and *-or* can also name *things* such as machines that perform certain operations or that can be used for certain purposes:

| | |
|---|---|
| grind, grinder | boil, boiler |
| mow, mower | reflect, reflector |
| wash, washer | sprinkle, sprinkler |

All of these examples add *-er* or *-or* to base words that have meaning in their own right. Now we will see some words that add the suffix *-or* to word *roots* from the Latin language. The suffix still names the person who does something, but the suffix is not added to independent base words. In the following list we have added the original Latin word to show you how it has been changed to fit the English language.

doctor (Latin *doctus*; from *docere*, to teach)
author (Latin *auctor*, one who originates something)
sculptor (from Latin *sculpere*, to carve)
ancestor (Latin *antecessor*, one that goes before)
proprietor (from Latin *proprietas*, property)

### ■ 10 e.2    *-ment*

In Section **10d** you saw the words *govern* and *government*. The suffix *-ment* names an act or a condition or the result of doing something, and it is often used to change verbs to nouns.

| | |
|---|---|
| pay, payment | encourage, encouragement |
| treat, treatment | punish, punishment |
| ship, shipment | judge, judgment (judgement) |
| enjoy, enjoyment | refresh, refreshment |

The suffix -*ment* can be added to most words without any change in spelling of the base word. This is because -*ment* begins with a consonant which does not conflict with the letter at the end of the base word. The word *judgment* is usually spelled without the final *e* in *judge*, although the spelling *judgement* is listed as an alternative in many dictionaries.

In all, there are at least two dozen suffixes that can be used to form nouns. In the following sections you will see some of the most important ones.

### ■ 10 e.3 -*ant* and -*ent*

The suffixes -*ant* and -*ent* are added to words to name the *person* or *thing* that performs an action. Often the base word is a verb. (Do not confuse the suffix -*ent* with -*ment*, which was just discussed in the preceding examples.)

| | |
|---|---|
| assist, assistant | occupy, occupant |
| attend, attendant | depend, dependent |
| contest, contestant | repel, repellent |
| descend, descendant | correspond, correspondent |

### ■ 10 e.4 -*ance* and -*ence*

The suffixes -*ance* and -*ence* can be added to verbs to name the state or quality of something or the process of doing something. Words ending with these prefixes often name the *result* of the action of the verb.

| | |
|---|---|
| admit, admittance | endure, endurance |
| appear, appearance | guide, guidance |
| assist, assistance | perform, performance |
| attend, attendance | resemble, resemblance |
| depend, dependence | correspond, correspondence |
| indulge, indulgence | occur, occurrence |

The final vowel in the base word is dropped because these suffixes also begin with vowels (*guide, guidance*).

With a few verbs, both the *-ant* and *-ance* suffixes can be used; with other verbs, both the *-ent* and *-ence* suffixes can be used.

> assist: assistant, assistance
> attend: attendant, attendance
>
> depend: dependent, dependence
> correspond: correspondent, correspondence

Remember that the suffixes *-ant* and *-ent* are used to name people or things that perform the action of the verb; plural forms of these nouns would end with *-ants* and *-ents*. On the other hand, the suffixes *-ance* and *-ence* name the process or the results of doing something. This will help you distinguish between plural nouns such as *assistants* (people who help) and singular nouns such as *assistance* (the act of helping).

### ■ 10 e.5 *-ion*

The suffix *-ion* is often used to change a verb to a noun that names the act of doing something or the result of doing something. When the *-ion* suffix is added to words ending with *t*, the ending sounds much like the word *shun*. The same is true when *ion* is added to words ending with *ss*.

> act, action          collect, collection
> elect, election       connect, connection
> invent, invention    prevent, prevention
> object, objection     protect, protection
> select, selection     reflect, reflection
>
> confess, confession   discuss, discussion
> depress, depression   impress, impression

As you know, many verbs end with *-ate*. The final *e* is dropped before *-ion* is added to change these verbs to nouns.

> dictate, dictation        communicate, communication
> donate, donation          concentrate, concentration
> locate, location          eliminate, elimination
> graduate, graduation      illustrate, illustration
> relate, relation          migrate, migration
> rotate, rotation          translate, translation

When *-ion* is added to words that end with letters other than *t* or *ss*, the final letter is often changed to *t* before *-ion* is added. Sometimes other letters in the word are changed or added to accept the *-ion* suffix. These words also have the *shun* sound for the suffix.

| | |
|---|---|
| attend, attention | describe, description |
| deceive, deception | intend, intention |
| receive, reception | subscribe, subscription |

Other words ending with *nd* change the final *d* to *s* before adding *-ion*. In these words the ending also has the *shun* sound.

| | |
|---|---|
| expand, expansion | comprehend, comprehension |
| extend, extension | suspend, suspension |

In some words that add *s* before the suffix *-ion*, the ending begins with a /zh/ sound (like the letter *s* in *vision*) rather than /sh/. Notice that the words ending with *de* or *t* change these letters to *s* before the suffix is added.

| | |
|---|---|
| confuse, confusion | convert, conversion |
| divide, division | invade, invasion |
| invert, inversion | provide, provision |

Some words cannot add the *-ion* suffix directly to the base word. These words need a connecting syllable that expands the suffix to *-ation*, but the meaning is the same as *-ion*.

| | |
|---|---|
| accuse, accusation | alter, alteration |
| combine, combination | consult, consultation |
| expect, expectation | install, installation |
| observe, observation | publish, publication |

Some verbs end with *-ify*. The final *y* is changed to *i* and a linking syllable is added to form the ending *-cation*.

| | |
|---|---|
| modify, modification | justify, justification |
| purify, purification | identify, identification |
| qualify, qualification | specify, specification |

**10**

### ■ 10 e.6    *-ism* and *-ist*

The suffix *-ism* creates a noun which names the act or process or system of doing something. The base word is often another noun, but sometimes it is an adjective.

| | |
|---|---|
| hero, heroism | critic, criticism |
| ideal, idealism | journal, journalism |
| manner, mannerism | modern, modernism |
| patriot, patriotism | skeptic, skepticism |

The suffix *-ist* names a person who does something or who follows a certain belief. Words ending with this suffix are often related to those ending with *-ism*. In the following list we have repeated some words ending with *-ism* to show how they can also add the suffix *-ist*.

| | |
|---|---|
| cello, cellist | journalism, journalist |
| copy, copyist | humor, humorist |
| idealism, idealist | modernism, modernist |
| physics, physicist | piano, pianist |
| science, scientist | solo, soloist |
| cello, cellist | violin, violinist |

Notice that the final *o* in *cello* and *piano* is dropped before *-ist* is added. Also notice the changes required in *physics* and *science* before this suffix is added.

### ■ 10 e.7    *-ness*

This suffix indicates a condition or the result of an action. The suffix *-ness* is often added to adjectives to create nouns.

| | |
|---|---|
| aware, awareness | bitter, bitterness |
| dark, darkness | happy, happiness |
| kind, kindness | quick, quickness |
| shy, shyness | still, stillness |
| weak, weakness | tender, tenderness |

Because the suffix begins with a consonant, the spelling of the base word does not change when *-ness* is added.

## ■ 10 e.8    *-ity, -ability, -ibility*

The suffix *-ity* means "quality or degree." It is often added to adjectives or verbs to create nouns.

| | |
|---|---|
| able, ability | celebrate, celebrity |
| dense, density | identify, identity |
| scarce, scarcity | necessary, necessity |

This suffix can also be added to adjectives that already end with the suffixes *-able* or *-ible* (See **10 f.2** below). In this case, the complete noun suffix becomes *-ability* or *-ibility*.

| | |
|---|---|
| readable, readability | responsible, responsibility |
| likable, likability | visible, visibility |
| usable, usability | eligible, eligibility |

## ■ 10 f    Adjective-Forming Suffixes

In Section **5g** you saw a number of suffixes that are often used to change a word from its original part of speech to an **adjective**. We will look at those suffixes more closely here.

## ▌ 10 f.1    *-y* and *-ly*

The suffix *-y* is often added to nouns to create adjectives. This suffix means "showing" or "suggesting." In some cases, adjectives such as *happy* and *heavy* exist independently and are not derived from a separate base word.

| | |
|---|---|
| happy | ease, easy |
| heavy | fun, funny |
| jolly | greed, greedy |
| merry | luck, lucky |
| dirt, dirty | rain, rainy |
| foam, foamy | snow, snowy |

The suffix *-ly* can be added to some nouns to create adjectives. (As you already saw in Section **6a**, *-ly* is more often used as an adverb suffix.)

| | |
|---|---|
| mother, motherly | heaven, heavenly |
| father, fatherly | scholar, scholarly |
| brother, brotherly | master, masterly |

## ▌ 10 f.2    *-able* and *-ible*

The suffixes *-able* and *-ible* mean "able to do something" or "capable of being something." These prefixes are often added to verbs or to nouns to change them to adjectives.

| | |
|---|---|
| read, readable | horror, horrible |
| break, breakable | permit, permissible |
| note, notable | respond, responsible |
| excuse, excusable | terror, terrible |
| value, valuable | love, lovable (*or* loveable) |
| detach, detachable | like, likable (*or* likeable) |
| present, presentable | use, usable (*or* useable) |

## ▌ 10 f.3    *-ic* and *-ish*

The suffixes *-ic* and *-ish* mean "having the characteristics of something." These suffixes are often added to nouns to create adjectives.

| | |
|---|---|
| frantic | geometry, geometric |
| authentic | strategy, strategic |
| base, basic | metal, metallic |
| hero, heroic | satire, satiric |

| | |
|---|---|
| boy, boyish | girl, girlish |
| child, childish | clown, clownish |
| self, selfish | snob, snobbish |

## ▌ 10 f.4    *-ful* and *-less*

The suffix *-ful* means "full of" or "having." (Notice that this suffix is spelled *-ful*, not *full*). It can be added to nouns or verbs to create adjectives.

| | |
|---|---|
| bashful | beauty, beautiful |
| grateful | plenty, plentiful |
| sorrow, sorrowful | tear, tearful |
| wonder, wonderful | youth, youthful |

The suffix *-less* means "without" or "lacking."

| | |
|---|---|
| cloud, cloudless | name, nameless |
| fault, faultless | effort, effortless |

As we have already seen, these two suffixes can be used to create *antonyms*: adjectives that mean the opposite of each other.

```
use     useful   -  useless
color   colorful -  colorless
faith   faithful -  faithless
help    helpful  -  helpless
hope    hopeful  -  hopeless
thank   thankful -  thankless
```

## ▌ 10f.5    *-ive*

This suffix is often added to verbs to derive adjectives. It means "tending toward" the action described by the verb. As you would expect, final *e* is dropped before *-ive* is added. Notice that some other words such as *decide* and *receive* also change the final consonant and other letters before this suffix is added.

```
act, active          adhere, adhesive
create, creative     decide, decisive
defend, defensive    destroy, destructive
offend, offensive    exhaust, exhaustive
select, selective    persuade, persuasive
receive, receptive   possess, possessive
```

## ▌ 10f.6    *-ant* and *-ent*

In Section **10e.3** you saw that these suffixes could be used to form *nouns*. They can also be used to form *adjectives*; they are sometimes added to verbs.

```
abundant              cohere, coherent
elegant               confide, confident
expect, expectant     consist, consistent
extravagant           depend, dependent
ignorant              diligent
important             excel, excellent
observe, observant    innocent
please, pleasant      intelligent
relevant              magnificent
reluctant             permanent
```

**10**

### ■ 10 f.7  *-an* and *-ian*

These suffixes mean "of" or "belonging to." They are often added to nouns to form adjectives. They are found especially in proper adjectives. Notice that the end of some base words is altered considerably before the suffix is added (*Norway, Norwegian*).

| | |
|---|---|
| Alaska, Alaskan | India, Indian |
| America, American | Norway, Norwegian |
| Canada, Canadian | Paris, Parisian |
| Mexico, Mexican | Peru, Peruvian |
| Rome, Roman | Shakespeare, Shakespearian |
| Tibet, Tibetan | Venice, Venetian |

These same words ending with *-an* and *-ian* can also be used as nouns in their own right.

They are from Canada. They are Canadian.
She is from Norway. She is a Norwegian.
He is from Alaska. He is an Alaskan.

### ■ 10 g  Verb-Forming Suffixes

A few suffixes can be added to nouns or adjectives to change them to verbs.

### ■ 10 g.1  *-ate*

This suffix means "become" or "cause to become." Sometimes this suffix can be added to base words to create verbs.

alien, alienate
pulse, pulsate
valid, validate

More often the *-ate* suffix is found at the end of verbs that originated in Latin. In that language, many verbs ended with *are*. This suffix changed to *-ate* when these words were taken into the English language. The original Latin verbs are given after the English words in the following list.

demonstrate (*demonstrare*)
designate (*designare*)
dictate (*dictare*)

elevate (*elevare*)
graduate (*graduare*)
illustrate (*illustrare*)
inflate (*inflare*)
locate (*locare*)
separate (*separare*)
vibrate (*vibrare*)

You saw in Section **10e.5** that the suffix *-ion* can be added to these words to form nouns (*locate, location*).

## ▌ 10g.2    *-en*

This suffix means "make" or "cause to become." It is often added to adjectives in order to form verbs.

| | |
|---|---|
| damp, dampen | bright, brighten |
| hard, harden | fright, frighten |
| sharp, sharpen | quick, quicken |

## ▌ 10g.3    *-ify*

This suffix means "cause" or "make." Notice that some word endings must be changed considerably in order to accept this suffix (*clear, clarify*; *terror, terrify*).

| | |
|---|---|
| beauty, beautify | identity, identify |
| clear, clarify | intense, intensify |
| just, justify | quality, qualify |
| unite, unify | simple, simplify |

## ▌ 10g.4    *-ize*

This suffix also means "make" or "cause to become."

| | |
|---|---|
| apology, apologize | authority, authorize |
| civil, civilize | critic, criticize |
| memory, memorize | familiar, familiarize |
| modern, modernize | sympathy, sympathize |

Final *y* in the base word changes to *i* (*memory, memorize*).

**10**

# *Check Your Understanding*

**Word Study**
*Answers begin on p. 299.*

Read the instructions very carefully for each question. You will be asked to use prefixes and suffixes in a number of ways. Sometimes the spellings in the given words are incorrect and you will be asked to correct them when you write the sentences.

If necessary, review the material in the sections indicated at the end of each question.

**1.** The following prefixes also mean "not": *in-, im-, il-, ir-.* Add one of these prefixes before the words written in boldface. Be sure to change the article if necessary. (10c.2)

    1. Most of his answers were **correct**.
    2. This handwriting is completely **legible**.
    3. They are often very **patient** while they are waiting.
    4. That was a **responsible** way to deal with the problem.

**2.** The following Latin prefixes originally meant "with" or "to-gether": *com-, col-, con-.* Add the appropriate form of this prefix in the blank space at the beginning of each word in boldface. (10c.3)

    1. They used signal lights to ___**municate** with the ship.
    2. May I ___**laborate** with someone on this project?
    3. I need to ___**centrate** on finishing my homework.
    4. Is the ___**mittee** going to have another meeting?

**3.** The Latin prefix *ad-* means "to" or "toward." It changes to *ac-, af, ap-, as-,* or *at-* before certain consonants. Look    at the list of words that begin with these prefixes, and then use the word that fits the blank in each of the following sentences. (10c.4)

    affect   approve   accept   assume   attend

    1. Please _____ my apology for the mistake.
    2. The bad weather will probably _____ their travel plans.
    3. Will you be able to _____ all the meetings?
    4. I hope they will _____ my application.
    5. You shouldn't _____ that things won't turn out well.

# *Check Your Understanding*

**4.** Each of the following words contains a prefix. After each word, write the prefix and the meaning of this prefix. (10c.7, 10c.8).
Here is an example:

proceed: *pro-* (forward, before)

| | |
|---|---|
| 1. supervise | 6. propose |
| 2. expel | 7. submerge |
| 3. implicate | 8. immigrant |
| 4. extravagant | 9. attract |
| 5. intermediate | 10. suppose |

**5.** Write the word that fits each of the following definitions. Each word should begin with the prefix *uni-*, *bi-*, *tri-*, *dec-*, or *cent-*. (10c.9)

1. Able to speak two languages:
2. A figure with ten sides:
3. Containing three parts:
4. One hundred years:
5. A thing formed by joining several things into one:
6. Consisting of two parts:

**6.** The Suffixes *-er* and *-ment* can be used to change verbs to nouns. Use the appropriate suffix after each of the verbs printed in boldface in the following sentences (10e.1, 10e.2):

1. He'll probably be late because he is a heavy **sleep**.
2. We haven't yet received **pay** for that **ship**.
3. She is a good **golf** and an excellent **swim**.
4. The **treat** has helped him to recover completely.

**7.** The suffixes *-ant* and *-ent* can be added to some verbs to change them to nouns. Add the appropriate suffix to each word in boldface in the following sentences (10e.3).

1. He was a **correspond** for a big newspaper.
2. The **occupy** of the room has already left.
3. The scientist and his **assist** discovered the vaccine.
4. Will this insect **repel** keep the bugs away?

**10**

# *Check Your Understanding*

**8.** Add the noun suffix *-ion* to each of the following words. Remember that the final letters of some words must be altered before this suffix is added (10e.5).

| | | | |
|---|---|---|---|
| 1. | rotate | 5. | protect |
| 2. | collect | 6. | discuss |
| 3. | attend | 7. | translate |
| 4. | invent | 8. | receive |

**9.** Add the adjective suffix *-ive* to each of the following verbs. Remember that the end of some verbs must be changed considerably to accept this suffix (10f.5).

1. create
2. defend
3. select
4. receive
5. decide
6. persuade

# Punctuation Guide

**APOSTROPHE (')**

> • The apostrophe is used to create possessive nouns that show who owns something.

▼ **Singular possessive nouns** end with the apostrophe and the letter *s* (*'s*).

> One *student's* composition won a prize.
> This *writer's* latest book is very good.
> The *box's* contents remained a mystery.

▼ **Plural possessive nouns** usually add only an apostrophe at the end of the regular plural form. This is because most plural nouns already end with *s* or *es*.

> Most of the students' papers were finished on time.
> Several of the writers' books won awards.
> Three of the boxes' labels were illegible.

▼ A few **irregular plural nouns** do not end with *s*. With these plural nouns, add *'s* to form the possessive.

> All of the *women's* coats are in the closet.
> The *people's* views were expressed at the meeting.
> Some *children's* parents met them after school.

> • Apostrophes are also used with verbs to create contractions that combine two words into one. The apostrophe takes the place of the letter or letters left out of one of the words.

## Punctuation Guide

▼ **Contractions** often consist of a verb followed by the adverb *not*. An apostrophe usually takes the place of the *o* in *not* when these words are written as contractions.

| | |
|---|---|
| don't (do not) | can't (can not) |
| isn't (is not) | wasn't (was not) |
| aren't (are not) | weren't (were not) |
| haven't (have not) | hadn't (had not) |
| doesn't (does not) | wouldn't (would not) |
| didn't (did not) | couldn't (could not) |
| won't (will not) | shouldn't (should not) |

When *can not* is written as a contraction, the apostrophe takes the place of the first two letters in *not*. Also notice that *will not* changes to *won't* when it is written as a contraction.

▼ Contractions may involve a pronoun followed by the shortened form of a verb. The verbs *be*, *have*, and *will* are often used in contractions of this type. The apostrophe takes the place of one or two letters in each of these verbs.

| | |
|---|---|
| I'm (I am) | we're (we are) |
| you're (you are) | they're (they are) |
| he's (he is) | she's (she is) |
| it's (it is) | |

| | |
|---|---|
| I've (I have) | we've (we have) |
| you've (you have) | they've (they have) |
| he's (he has) | she's (she has) |
| it's (it has) | |

| | |
|---|---|
| I'd (I had) | we'd (we had) |
| you'd (you had) | they'd (they had) |
| he'd (he had) | she'd (she had) |
| it'd (it had) | |

| | |
|---|---|
| I'll (I will) | we'll (we will) |
| you'll (you will) | they'll (they will) |
| he'll (he will) | she'll (she will) |
| it'll (it will) | |

▼ Contractions can be formed by shortening the verb after interrogative pronouns (*who*, *what*) and after adverbs that introduce questions (*how*, *when*, *where*). The verbs *be* and *will* are often used this way.

> **How's** it going? (**How is** it going?)
> **Who's** at the door? (**Who is** at the door?)
> **What's** the answer? (**What is** the answer?)
> **When's** he going to meet us? (**When is** he going to meet us?)
> **Where's** my other glove? (**Where is** my other glove?)
> **Who'll** pick me up? (**Who will** pick me up?)
> **What'll** I do then? (**What will** I do then?)

▼ Sometimes a verb can be joined with a noun to form a contraction. The verb *be* is often used this way.

> **Ellen's** going with us. (**Ellen is** going with us.)
> **Ed's** working in the yard. (**Ed is** working in the yard.)
> The **dog's** chasing a squirrel. (The **dog is** chasing a squirrel.)

The words *Ellen's*, *Ed's*, and *dog's* look like *possessive nouns*, but notice that each noun is followed by a verb ending with *-ing*. This verb form is called the **present participle**. Verb phrases such as *is going*, *is working*, and *is chasing* are examples of the **present progressive.** In this form, the helping verb *be* is followed by a present participle, which provides the *main verb*.

COLON (:)

▼ The colon is used between the hour and the minute when the time is written in numbers.

> It is now 10:15 a.m.
> The movie starts at 7:30 p.m.

Notice that **a.m.** and **p.m.** are written with periods (not **am** and **pm**). Look at the entry for the **period** to see why this is so.

▼ The colon is used after the salutation in a formal letter.

Dear Sir or Madam:
Dear Mrs. Evans:
Dear Dr. Williams:

▼ The colon is used to introduce a list of items at the end of a sentence. Usually the beginning of the sentence will contain a phrase such as *the following*.

Our supply closet contains the following items: four staplers, three rolls of tape, two pairs of scissors, and six boxes of paper clips.

**COMMA (,)**

▼ Commas are used to separate three or more items in a series.

Snakes, turtles, and lizards are cold-blooded animals.
The zoo just got some camels, zebras, elephants, and kangaroos.
We went to Washington, Philadelphia, and New York.

▼ The comma should be used to separate two adjectives if both adjectives are of equal importance and if their order could be reversed.

He can be a stubborn, difficult person.
He can be a difficult, stubborn person.

Do not use a comma to separate two adjectives before a noun if the adjectives work together and if they would not make sense in reverse order.

I found a *big brown* spider under that rock.
The *little gray* mouse was hiding in the corner.

▼ Commas separate the two parts of a compound sentence. The comma is placed just before the coordinating conjunctions *and*, *or*, or *but*.

> We got the car repaired, and we completed the trip without any more problems.
>
> You can finish the ice cream now, or you can save some for later.
>
> He worked very hard, but he didn't finish before the rain started.

▼ Commas are used to set off brief introductory parts of a sentence. These are usually interjections or names used in direct address.

> Well, I'm glad that job is finished.
>
> So, you finally got here.
>
> Allen, please bring me some more ketchup.
>
> Kim, will you see who is at the door?

▼ A comma is used at the end of a *dependent clause* when it begins the sentence.

> After the storm ended, we went out to look at the damage.
>
> Before we leave, we should be sure we've got everything we will need.

**EXCLAMATION MARK (!)**

An exclamation mark is used at the end of an exclamatory sentence that expresses surprise or anger or some other strong feeling.

> I never want to go through that again!
>
> This room is an unbelievable mess!

An exclamation mark may also be used after an interjection at the beginning of a sentence. This helps to make the effect of the interjection stronger than it would be if a comma were used.

> Ouch! That really hurt!
> Oh NO! You didn't really do that, did you?

**HYPHEN (-)**

▼ The hyphen connects the parts of some compound words.

| | |
|---|---|
| baby-sit | push-ups |
| great-grandmother | great-grandfather |
| mother-in-law | father-in-law |
| runner-up | by-product |
| merry-go-round | front-runner |

When compound numbers from twenty-one through ninety-nine are written out, the hyphen should be used.

| | |
|---|---|
| thirty-two | fifty-seven |
| eighty-five | ninety-three |

▼ When compound words are used as adjectives just before nouns, these adjectives are often hyphenated. This is especially true with adjectives beginning with the word *well*.

> They are *well-known* performers.
> That was a *fast-paced* movie.

▼ When these compound adjectives appear after the noun they modify, the hyphen is not used.

> They are performers who are well known.

▼ If you want to divide a long word between two lines, then use a hyphen between syllables. Words containing only one syllable are never divided, and longer words should be hyphenated according to their syllable patterns.

Some words contain doubled consonants which often appear at the end of stressed short-vowel syllables. In words of this type, place the hyphen between the consonants:

but-ter, mid-dle, col-lar, rab-bit, chal-lenge

In many other words, one syllable ends with a consonant and the next syllable begins with a different consonant. Place the hyphen between the consonants in words such as these:

lum-ber, fin-ger, spar-kle, for-tune

When one syllable ends with a long vowel and the next syllable begins with a consonant, place the hyphen between the long vowel and the consonant:

la-bor, fi-nal, no-tice, ru-mor

You know that many words begin with prefixes and end with suffixes. Place the hyphen so that the structure of the word is clear: prefix-root-suffix. When a suffix begins with a consonant, the hyphen is placed just before this consonant.

in-crease, ex-press, con-clude, at-tract
use-ful, worth-less, pay-ment, kind-ness

Use your knowledge of base words and roots to help you decide how to hyphenate long words. This information, combined with your knowledge of prefixes and suffixes, will usually help you determine the logical way to hyphenate words such as these when they appear at the end of a line:

com-municate, commu-nicate, communi-cate
in-complete, incom-plete
en-chantment, enchant-ment
com-puter, comput-er

When you need to divide a long word at the end of a line, do not guess where to put the hyphen. If you are not sure, then check your dictionary.

**PERIOD (.)**

▼ The period is used at the end of **declamatory sentences** and **imperative sentences**.

> I don't know where the time went.
> Please close the door when you leave.

▼ The period is used with **abbreviations** to show that some letters have been omitted from words.

| | |
|---|---|
| Mr. (Mister) | Sun. (Sunday) |
| Mrs. (Mistress) | Tues. (Tuesday) |
| Ave. (Avenue) | Jan. (January) |
| St. (Street) | Nov. (November) |

When we write the time we use the abbreviations **a.m.** and **p.m.**, which must always include a period after each letter: 9:15 a.m., 6:30 p.m. This is because **a.m.** is an abbreviation for the Latin words *ante meridiem* (before noon) and *p.m.* is an abbreviation for *post meridiem* (after noon).

**QUESTION MARK (?)**

The question mark is used at the end of **interrogative sentences**.

> Where have you been?
> Who was on the phone?
> How much more pizza can you eat?

**QUOTATION MARKS (" ")**

Quotation marks are used to show who is speaking when you write **dialogue**: a conversation between two or more people. *Quotation marks are always used in pairs.*

▼ Place one quotation mark before the first spoken word and another quotation mark after the last spoken word.

▼ The word just after the first quotation mark is always capitalized.

▼ If the spoken passage begins with words such as *He said* or *She asked*, place a comma after these words just before the first quotation mark.

▼ If the spoken passage comes at the end of the sentence, then place the end punctuation inside the quotation mark.
> He said, "I think I'd better leave now."
> She asked, "How much longer do we have to wait?"

▼ If words such as *he said* or *she said* appear after the spoken passage, then a comma is usually placed before the last quotation mark.
> "It's time to leave," he said.
> "I don't know where he is," she replied.

▼ If the spoken passage is a **question** or an **exclamation**, then the question mark or the exclamation mark is used as punctuation just before the last quotation mark. The complete sentence ends with a period.
> "Watch out for that low branch!" she shouted.
> "When will you be ready to leave?" he asked.

▼ When you write dialogue, begin a new paragraph each time the speaker changes. Also use only one set of quotation marks when one person speaks several sentences in a row.

> "When can we leave?" whined Robert.
> "We will leave when everything is ready," replied Dad.
> Mom said, "We can't leave now because I have to feed the cat and take the dog for a walk. Dad has to make sure all the windows are closed, and you still have to clean up your room."
> "Well, maybe we shouldn't plan to leave before tomorrow," said Dad as he retrieved a roller skate from the kitchen cabinet.

### SEMICOLON (;)

The semicolon can be used to separate the two parts of a compound sentence. When this is done, the semicolon takes the place of a conjunction such as *and*, *or*, or *but*. The semicolon shows that the two parts of the sentence are of equal importance.

> They wanted to play baseball; I wanted to go swimming.
> Maria went to the movie; Ellen went shopping.

# Chapter 1: Sentences

*Answers for questions on page 16.*

**Sentences**

1. Mistakes in these **declarative** and **interrogative** sentences are corrected in boldface.

   1. **Is** this the one you're looking for**?**
   2. **My** little sister is five and my brother is seven.
   3. **W**here did you leave all the stuff I gave you**?**
   4. **My** family is going on a trip to Fresno and Los Angeles.
   5. **A**re these the only raccoons you have**?**

2. Mistakes in these **imperative** and **exclamatory** sentences are corrected in boldface.

   1. **W**atch out for the thin ice!
   2. **P**lease don't make so much noise.
   3. **I** couldn't believe he made that catch!
   4. **J**ust leave the packages on the table.
   5. **T**hat was the most fun **I** ever had!

3. These sentences are changed so that each question becomes a statement and each statement becomes a question. The order of the subject and predicate in each sentence is reversed, and end punctuation is altered.

   1. **They are going** to leave tomorrow.
   2. **Is he** one of the best students in class**?**
   3. **This is** a good book about space travel.
   4. **Have they** already gone back home**?**
   5. **I should** write a story about a monster from space.

# Chapter 1: Sentences

*Answers for questions on page 17.*

**Subjects and Predicates**

1. A short line is drawn between the **complete subject** and the **complete predicate** in each sentence. Also, the *simple subject* and the *simple predicate* are underlined.

    1. Yesterday we | drove up to see my grandparents.
    2. The players on my team | are all very good.
    3. One day I | met a purple space creature on the bus.
    4. Finally they | reached the end of their journey.
    5. The first question | was the most difficult of all.

2. The presence of a **compound subject** *or* a **compound predicate** is indicated in each sentence. Also the words that make up each subject or predicate are written.

    1. In the summer I swim a lot and play baseball every day.
       Compound predicate: swim and play
    2. My friends and I are going camping this summer
       Compound subject: friends and I
    3. Snakes and lizards are not my favorite animals.
       Compound subject: Snakes and lizards
    4. My dog ran away from me and chased a squirrel.
       Compound predicate: ran and chased
    5. Susan and Ellen went to the circus together.
       Compound subject: Susan and Ellen

3. Parts of short sentences are combined into a single sentence containing a **compound subject** or a **compound predicate**.

    1. We went to New York and saw the Statue of Liberty.
    2. Evan and I play on the team.
    3. They stood at the window and watched the storm raging.
    4. Kate and her friend went to the movies.
    5. My friend called and asked me to come to her house.

# *Chapter 1: Sentences*

*Answers for questions on page 18.*

**Simple and Compound Sentences**

1. A short line is drawn between the subject and predicate of **each part** of these compound sentences.

    1. Kay | wanted to see a movie, but she | played soccer instead.
    2. We | wandered through the woods, and we | saw some chipmunks.
    3. Both boys | play football, and they | are very good.
    4. Some people | like the mountains, but others | prefer the beach.
    5. They | arrived last Monday, and they | stayed for three days.

2. Each pair of original simple sentences is rewritten to form a compound sentence.

    1. Fred is really a cat, but he acts like a person.
    2. Ellen liked the book, and I liked it, too.
    3. I wanted to go bowling, but we went to a movie instead.
    4. He was not very big, but he played football anyway.
    5. My family went to California, and we had a good time.

3. Changes are made so that pairs of sentences are combined into compound sentences.

    1. He fell down at the beginning of the race, but he still won.
    2. We ran down the stairs, and we raced out the door.
    3. They went to New York, and they visited their relatives.
    4. The trip was fun, but I was glad when it was over.
    5. We can stay a little longer, or we can leave now.

# Chapter 2: Nouns

*Answers for questions on page 33.*

**Singular and Plural Nouns**

1. Each singular noun in the original list is rewritten in its **plural** form.

   1. mailboxes       6. territories
   2. supplies        7. ambushes
   3. berries         8. associates
   4. crutches        9. journeys
   5. apologies      10. directors

2. Each singular noun is rewritten in its **plural** form.

   1. potatoes        6. radios
   2. leaves          7. cliffs
   3. children        8. women
   4. shelves         9. volcanos
   5. tomatoes       10. pianos

3. All the nouns in each sentence are underlined.

   1. The <u>river</u> wound through the <u>canyon</u> to the <u>sea</u>.

   2. All the <u>owls</u> and <u>hawks</u> were hunting for <u>rabbits</u> and <u>mice</u>.

   3. The <u>porch</u>, the <u>roof</u>, and the <u>garage</u> were badly damaged.

   4. Our <u>journey</u> began by <u>car</u> and continued by <u>ship</u> and <u>plane</u>.

   5. <u>Engineers</u> designed a <u>tunnel</u> through the <u>mountain</u>.

# Chapter 2: Nouns

*Answers for questions on page 34.*

**Common and Proper Nouns; Nouns in a Series**

**1.** Each common noun is underlined once and each proper noun is underlined twice.

    1.   Holland and Belgium are neighboring countries.

    2.   Dolphins and whales are found in the Pacific Ocean.

    3.   The continents of Europe and Asia are connected.

    4.   Get out the overcoats and snowshoes before winter arrives.

    5.   All the plates and glasses are on the shelf.

**2.** Commas and the word *and* are added to clarify these sentences containing nouns in a series.

    1.   The room was filled with sofas, chairs, tables, and lamps.
    2.   My brothers, sisters, and friends all came to my party.
    3.   Where are my books, papers, and pencils?
    4.   The storm blew twigs, leaves, and paper into the yard.
    5.   We saw horses, elephants, clowns, and acrobats at the circus.

# Chapter 2: Nouns

*Answers for questions on page 34.*

**Possessive Nouns**

1.  These sentences use the **possessive** form of each noun originally given in parentheses.

    1.  One **car's** left front fender was damaged.
    2.  Both **planes'** pilots were in the air show.
    3.  This **knife's** blade is not sharp enough to cut the rope.
    4.  All three of my **friends'** parents were at the meeting.
    5.  This brown **bear's** paws are extremely large.

2.  The singular possessive *and* the plural possessive form of each noun is written.

    monkey's, monkeys'        woman's, women's
    person's, people's        house's, houses'
    holiday's, holidays'      volcano's, volcanoes'
    country's, countries'     journey's, journeys'

# *Chapter 3: Pronouns*

*Answers for questions on page 56.*

### Using Indefinite Pronouns

**1.** This list of indefinite pronouns was given:

    most    somebody    anyone    all    everyone

One of these indefinite pronouns is used to take the place of each group of words printed in boldface in the original sentences.

1. **Everyone** cheered when he hit a home run.
2. Did **anyone** see what happened here?
3. **Most** of the wall collapsed.
4. **All** of the players on the team got a hit.
5. **Somebody** in the room left the window open.

**2.** Here is another list of indefinite pronouns:

    neither    several    both    anyone    everyone

One of these pronouns is used in each sentence below.

1. Does **anyone** know where Tom is?
2. I scraped **both** of my knees on the sidewalk.
3. Be sure that **everyone** gets a copy of the instructions.
4. **Neither** of the two bicycles was in good condition.
5. **Several** of the students brought pictures to school.

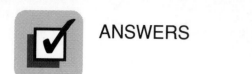 

# Chapter 3: Pronouns

*Answers for questions on pages 57, 58.*

**Subject and Object Pronouns**

1. Each sentence is rewritten using a *personal pronoun* as the **subject** in place of the nouns in the original sentences.

   1. **He** rode by in his royal carriage.
   2. **She** lived in a small town on the coast of Maine.
   3. **They** cheered when their team won the game.
   4. **It** needs to be repaired.
   5. **We** hurried home after school.

2. A *personal pronoun* is used as the **object** in place of the nouns in the original sentences.

   1. We gave a party for **her**.
   2. I saw some of **them** downtown last Saturday.
   3. Please put **it** on the table over there.
   4. I played baseball with **him** yesterday.
   5. The teacher asked **us** to get some supplies.

**The Antecedent of the Pronoun**

An arrow is drawn from each pronoun back to the noun that is its **antecedent**.

1. Sometimes my dreams don't come true, but sometimes **they** do.

2. The team got better and better, and **it** won lots of games.

3. My dog is not very big, but **he** makes a lot of noise.

4. My friends and I went to a movie, and then **we** took the bus back home.

5. Cindy didn't know that **she** had won first prize in the contest.

# Chapter 3: Pronouns

*Answers for questions on page 58.*

**Using Pronouns with Nouns**

1. Corrections are made in the pronouns that are used with nouns.

   1. **We students** were glad when vacation began.
   2. The teacher let **us boys** go out at recess.
   3. **We swimmers** won a trophy last year.
   4. They gave **us girls** a chance to play volleyball.

2. Changes are made in the pronouns that were used incorrectly in the original sentences.

   1. **Ed and I** couldn't wait for the game to start.
   2. They wanted to give Ellen and **me** a nice present.
   3. **He and I** were supposed to be next in line.
   4. He said he tried to call Tom and **me** four times.
   5. This package came for Sarah and **me**.

# Chapter 3: Pronouns

*Answers for questions on page 59.*

**Possessive Pronouns**

1. The correct **possessive pronouns** are used in place of the pronouns that were given in parentheses in the original sentences.

   1. Please give Susan **her** books.
   2. I think this is **their** dog.
   3. Evan lost **his** watch somewhere on the playground.
   4. I saw **your** brother when I was at the store.
   5. One of the tractors lost **its** steering wheel.

2. The pronouns in parentheses were not correct in the original sentences. These words have been changed so that they become **possessive pronouns** that can stand alone.

   1. That pencil must be **yours**.
   2. Are these coats **ours**?
   3. I don't know which hat is **hers**.
   4. I believe this desk is **his**.
   5. These chairs must be **theirs**.

3. These possessive pronouns were listed:

   theirs   yours   mine   ours   hers

   One of these pronouns is used in place of the words in italics in the original sentences.

   1. Her books are over there. I can't find **mine** anywhere.
   2. His shoes are soaked. Did **yours** get wet, too?
   3. Our leaves are all raked. Have they raked **theirs** yet?
   4. John's cap is over there. Where is **hers**?
   5. Their house has been painted. **Ours** will be painted tomorrow.

# *Chapter 3: Pronouns*

*Answers for questions on page 60.*

### Using *Who, Whom,* and *Whose*

1. The pronouns **who**, **whom**, or **whose** are used to fit each blank space in the original sentences.

     1. Find out **who** is at the door.
     2. **Whose** bike is standing out in the rain?
     3. **Whom** should I see when I get there?
     4. I'm not sure **whose** books these are.
     5. **Who** is waiting to see me?
     6. By **whom** was the speech given?

2. Each of the original sentences began with *who* and ended with a preposition. The sentences are rewritten so that the correct pronoun *whom* is used. The order of words is changed so that the prepositions *for, with, by, to,* and *from* come before the pronoun.

     1. **For whom** were they asking?
     2. **With whom** are you going to the game?
     3. **By whom** was the package delivered?
     4. **To whom** was this letter addressed?
     5. **From whom** did you get that idea?

# *Chapter 4: Verbs*

*Answers for questions on page 88.*

**The Verb Tenses**

1.  In each of these sentences a verb was given in its base form in parentheses. Here the verb is used in the **present tense** in each sentence.

    1.  He **is** one of my best friends.
    2.  My cat **chases** his tail all day.
    3.  She **has** a notebook just like mine.
    4.  His mom **encourages** him in everything he does.
    5.  This port **receives** many ships every day.

2.  The original sentences also gave verbs in the base form. Here each verb is used in the **past tense**.

    1.  Last summer we **traveled** to Idaho and Montana.
    2.  Yesterday I **was** caught in a big storm.
    3.  Last week we **visited** my grandparents.
    4.  Last month we **had** a good time at the beach.
    5.  I **stumbled** in the dark and **bruised** my toe last night.

3.  The original sentences all showed the base form of verbs in parentheses. Here each verb is used in the **future tense**.

    1.  Tomorrow I **will go** to the dentist.
    2.  Next week we **will exhibit** our pictures in the gallery.
    3.  They **will launch** the weather balloon next Tuesday.
    4.  My uncle **will arrive** some time next week.
    5.  I hope the teacher **will explain** how to solve this problem.

# *Chapter 4: Verbs*

*Answers for questions on page 89.*

### Action Verbs and Direct Objects

1.  Each of these sentences contains an **action verb** and a **direct object**. The action verb is underlined once and the direct object is underlined twice. Then a diagram shows the subject, the verb, and the direct object.

    1.  The postman <u>delivered</u> a <u>package</u> to us yesterday.

        | postman | delivered | package |

    2.  Leon <u>dropped</u> his <u>watch</u> into the mud.

        | Leon | dropped | watch |

    3.  The flood <u>covered</u> many <u>roads</u> in the county.

        | flood | covered | roads |

    4.  Yesterday we <u>watched</u> a <u>movie</u> about snakes and lizards.

        | we | watched | movie |

    5.  Divers <u>located</u> the <u>ship</u> under eighty feet of water.

        | Divers | located | ship |

# Chapter 4: Verbs

*Answers for questions on pages 89, 90.*

**Main Verbs; Helping Verbs; Linking Verbs**

2.  Each of these sentences contains a **helping verb** followed by the **main verb**. The helping verb is underlined *once*, and the main verb is underlined *twice*. (p. 89)

    1.  I am going to Denver next summer.

    2.  He had mowed the whole lawn before the rain started.

    3.  This winter has been unusually cold and wet.

    4.  We are planning a trip to Washington and New York.

    5.  She is working on a science project.

    6.  We have waited a long time for this game.

---

1.  These sentences all contain **linking verbs**. Each linking verb is underlined once. Then each sentence is rewritten using a *different* linking verb. (p. 90)

    1.  The water was very cold.

        The water **felt** very cold.

    2.  That book seems interesting and amusing.

        That book **is** interesting and amusing.

    3.  Our new neighbors are very friendly.

        Our new neighbors **seem** very friendly.

    4.  The dog looked wet and shaggy after the rain.

        The dog **appeared** wet and shaggy after the rain.

    5.  They were very nervous as the storm approached.

        They **seemed** very nervous as the storm approached.

# *Chapter 4: Verbs*

*Answers for questions on page 90.*

2. Each of these sentences contains a **linking verb** and a **predicate noun**. The linking verb is underlined once and the predicate noun is underlined twice. The diagram shows the subject, the verb, and the predicate noun.

1. Maria's dad is a jet pilot.

   dad | is \ pilot

2. Thomas Jefferson was the third president of the United States.

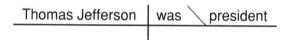

   Thomas Jefferson | was \ president

3. My math teacher is also a baseball coach in the summer.

   teacher | is \ coach

4. Ms. Roberts became our new mayor last month.

   Ms. Roberts | became \ mayor

5. Ellen was the winner of the first prize.

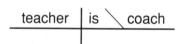

   Ellen | was \ winner

6. I am the captain of our team.

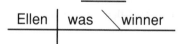

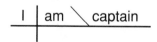

   I | am \ captain

# Chapter 4: Verbs

*Answers for questions on page 91.*

**Contractions; Agreement between Subject and Verb**

1. These sentences originally contained a verb followed by the word *not*. Here, a contraction that combines the verb with the word *not* is used.

   1. I **don't** know where he went.
   2. They **aren't** at home and I can not locate them.
   3. I **haven't** seen him all day.
   4. Ellen and Maria **weren't** in school yesterday.
   5. The workers **hadn't** finished the job before the rain began.

2. These sentences contain a pronoun followed by a verb. Here a contraction that combines the pronoun with the verb is used.

   1. **I'm** sure he will be back soon.
   2. **We're** going to the mountains next summer.
   3. **They've** been looking for their dog all day.
   4. **He's** one of my best friends.
   5. **She'd** been traveling for three days.

3. In the original sentences the subject and verb did not agree. Here the **verb** is changed so that it agrees with the subject.

   1. The students in my class **are** going to take a trip.
   2. John and Frank **were** the best players on the team.
   3. He always **has** a lot of fun at his cousin's house.
   4. The men standing on the corner **were** waiting for the bus.
   5. The people who live next door **have** two dogs and a cat.

# *Chapter 5: Adjectives*

*Answers to questions on pages 112, 113.*

**Using Adjectives**

1.  The correct adjective is chosen from those given in parentheses in the original sentences.

    1.  We had **a** very good time.
    2.  This is **an** unexpected development.
    3.  Have you heard about **this** discovery?
    4.  We will use **that** chemical in the experiment.
    5.  **These** keys have been missing for a week.

2.  These sentences were originally written with a noun preceded by an adjective near the end of the sentence. They have been rewritten so that the noun comes near the beginning and the adjective is moved to the end of the sentence to become a **predicate adjective**.

    1.  Those trees are extremely old.
    2.  That test was very easy.
    3.  These rings and bracelets are expensive.
    4.  This piece of pie is delicious.
    5.  That trip was unusually long.

    Each of the five sentences originally began with a demonstrative pronoun. These words became demonstrative adjectives when the sentences were rewritten (*Those* trees, *That* test, and so on).

3.  In the original sentences, some words were written in parentheses. The appropriate suffix is added here to change these words to adjectives.

    1.  That was a **lucky** break for you.
    2.  He is one of the most **famous** performers on television.
    3.  These flowers are very **beautiful**.
    4.  We had a **wonderful** time at the party.
    5.  This was one of the most **enjoyable** movies I have seen.

# Chapter 5: Adjectives

*Answers to questions on page 113.*

**4.** The predicate adjective in each sentence is underlined. Then the diagram shows the **subject**, the **verb**, and the **predicate adjective**.

1. The water became very <u>hot</u> in the sunlight.

   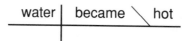

   water | became \ hot

2. They seemed <u>happy</u> after winning the game.

   They | seemed \ happy

3. The sailors were <u>fortunate</u> to escape the storm.

   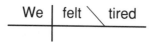

   sailors | were \ fortunate

4. We felt extremely <u>tired</u> after the long walk.

   We | felt \ tired

5. I was <u>glad</u> when the test was over.

   I | was \ glad

6. The runners appeared <u>exhausted</u> after the race.

   runners | appeared \ exhausted

# *Chapter 5: Adjectives*

*Answers to questions on page 114.*

**Making Comparisons with Adjectives**

1. The suffixes *er* or *est* are added to write the **comparative form** or the **superlative form** of adjectives originally given in parentheses.

   1. This is the **largest** dinosaur ever discovered.
   2. We need a **bigger** hammer for these large nails.
   3. Isn't this tree **taller** than that one?
   4. I just saw the **ugliest** alligator in the world!

2. The word *more* or *most* is added to write the **comparative form** or the **superlative form** of each adjective originally given in parentheses.

   1. This coat is **more practical** than that one.
   2. That was the **most important** decision he ever made.
   3. I was **more afraid** than he was.
   4. That was the **most interesting** book I ever read.

3. The **comparative form** or the **superlative form** is used for each adjective originally given in its base form

   1. This movie was **worse** than the one we saw last week.
   2. Who has the **best** team in the league?
   3. He ate **more** cookies than I did.
   4. He scored the **most** points of anybody on the team.

# *Chapter 5: Adjectives*

*Answers to questions on page 115.*

**Adjectives in a Series; Proper Adjectives**

**1.** Commas are added to make each series of adjectives clear to the reader. Words such as *and* or *or* are added when needed.

1. The small, heavy statue was made of marble.
2. The game was long, slow, dull, and tiresome.
3. We had some red, ripe, delicious tomatoes.
4. All the speakers were bright, witty, and clever.
5. The brief, intense storm did a lot of damage.

**2.** Each proper noun in the original is changed to a **proper adjective**.

1. The **Swedish** coastline has many small inlets called *fjords*.
2. Many **Roman** fountains were built centuries ago.
3. The **Russian** language is very different from the **English** language.
4. The **African** continent is home to many different animals.
5. A large **Mexican** hat is called a *sombrero*.

# Chapter 6. Adverbs

*Answers to questions on page 132.*

**Adverbs That Modify Verbs, Adjectives, and Adverbs**

1. Words originally given in parentheses are changed to **adverbs**, and an arrow is drawn from the adverb to the **verb** it modifies.

   1. He ran **quickly** toward us.

   2. We watched him very **carefully**.

   3. They **usually** leave home at seven-thirty.

   4. The storm blew up **suddenly** from the west.

   5. We trudged **slowly** through the mud.

2. The **adverb** in each sentence is underlined and an arrow is drawn from the adverb to the **adjective** it modifies.

   1. This turned out to be an <u>unusually</u> difficult job.

   2. That movie was <u>completely</u> ridiculous.

   3. We waited an <u>extremely</u> long time for the bus.

   4. There was a <u>very</u> large tree lying across the road.

   5. The stone was <u>too</u> heavy for us to move.

3. An arrow is drawn from the adverb in boldface to the word it modifies. There is also an indication of the part of speech of the modified word: verb, adjective, or another adverb.

   1. The missing watch appeared **unexpectedly**. (verb)

   2. Isn't it **unusually** early to be leaving for school? (adjective)

   3. They played **extremely** well in the last game. (adverb)

   4. The **slightly** damaged books were on sale at low prices. (adjective)

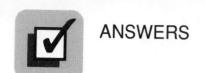 

# *Chapter 6. Adverbs*

*Answers to questions on page 133.*

**Using Adverbs Correctly**

**1.** The correct word is chosen from those given in parentheses.

1. Did they play as **well** as you hoped they would?
2. We traveled **farther** than they did.
3. The movie was **really** enjoyable.
4. I didn't find **any** of the books you wanted.
5. She sang very **well** in the concert.

**2.** Adverbs are written in the **comparative** or **superlative** degrees, as required.

1. This kite flies much **better** than that one.
2. I believe this is the **most unusual** fossil in the museum.
3. This skateboard runs much **worse** than the other one.
4. I hope this test is **easier** than the last one.
5. This was judged the **most beautiful** flower in the show.

**3.** Mistakes in each sentence are corrected in boldface.

1. We didn't see **anybody** we knew.
2. He's the **worst** baseball player I ever saw.
3. My brother is taller than I am, but I can run **faster**.
4. There wasn't **anything** we could do about it.
5. I thought they did a **really** good job.

# Chapter 7. Function Words

*Answers to questions on page 153.*

**Prepositions**

1.  Each complete prepositional phrase is underlined once. A second line is added under the preposition itself.

    1.  The scientists looked for the source of the radiation.
    2.  This novel by Dickens is set in England and in France.
    3.  Answers to your questions are in one chapter of this book.
    4.  Your gloves are on the chair beside the window.
    5.  For several years we have gone to the beach on vacation.

2.  Each complete prepositional phrase is underlined. An arrow is drawn from the phrase to the word it modifies. After each sentence there is an indication of which phrases function as **adjectives** and which phrases function as **adverbs**.

    1.  I raked the lawn before dark. (adverb)
    2.  The books on this shelf are all biographies. (adjective)
    3.  Please put this coat in the closet. (adverb)
    4.  After the game we went out to get pizza. (adverb)
    5.  The house across the street is being painted. (adjective)

3.  Each sentence is rewritten and corrected. Some prepositional phrases have been moved within the sentence, and each phrase is underlined. Verbs in boldface have been corrected.

    1.  Four of the students in my class have baby sisters.
    2.  The best one of these drinks **is** the grape soda.
    3.  We looked in three stores for boots with rubber soles.
    4.  Some kids in my school **are** on a little league team.

# Chapter 7. Function Words

*Answers to questions on page 154.*

**Conjunctions**

1. Short sentences are combined by using **coordinating conjunctions** *and, or,* or *but.*

   1. Ellen **and** Maria brought some colored leaves to class.
   2. We looked in a dozen magazines, **but** we didn't find the kind of photograph we wanted.
   3. We may go to a movie, **or** we may stay home and watch TV.
   4. Jaime likes math**, and** he is very good in science.
       OR: Jaime likes math **and** is very good in science.
   5. Kim made some cookies, **and** Sue brought some doughnuts.

2. Dependent clauses are underlined, and the **subordinating conjunction** that begins each clause is underlined a second time.

   1. <u>Because</u> it was raining so hard, we decided to stay inside.
   2. He got lost <u>when</u> he made a wrong turn.
   3. <u>After</u> we finish shopping, we will get something to drink.
   4. <u>Although</u> the weather was bad, we decided to go anyway.
   5. I managed to finish the test <u>before</u> the bell rang.

3. The two components of each **correlative conjunction** are underlined.

   1. Please bring <u>either</u> my raincoat <u>or</u> my umbrella.
   2. <u>Both</u> my sister <u>and</u> my aunt have birthdays this month.
   3. <u>If</u> you find a good photograph of the Grand Canyon, <u>then</u> please let me see it.
   4. He has <u>neither</u> cleaned his room <u>nor</u> finished his homework.
   5. The house was damaged <u>not only</u> by the wind <u>but also</u> by the flood.

# Chapter 8: More About Verbs

*Answers to questions on page 178.*

1. **Transitive and Intransitive Verbs**

   The verb in each sentence is underlined and marked **transitive** or **intransitive**.

   1. He plays the piano and the organ. (transitive)
   2. This car rides very smoothly. (intransitive)
   3. We heard the sound of rushing water. (transitive)
   4. The car hit a bump in the road. (transitive)
   5. She sings very well. (intransitive)

2. **Direct and Indirect Objects**

   Each **direct object** is underlined once, and each **indirect object** is underlined twice.

   1. We bought two new chairs for the kitchen.
   2. Mom and dad gave me some money for my birthday.
   3. I didn't see them at the game.
   4. We gave her the message you wanted delivered.
   5. They lost all their suitcases on the trip.

# Chapter 8: More About Verbs

*Answers to questions on page 179.*

### 3. Principal Parts of Regular Verbs

These verbs were listed in their base forms:

reserve   finish   discard   replace   impress

The four principal parts of each verb are written here:

| Present Tense | Present Participle | Past Tense | Past Participle |
|---|---|---|---|
| reserve, reserves | reserving | reserved | reserved |
| finish, finishes | finishing | finished | finished |
| discard, discards | discarding | discarded | discarded |
| replace, replaces | replacing | replaced | replaced |
| impress, impresses | impressing | impressed | impressed |

### 4. Active Voice and Passive Voice

Each sentence is labelled ACTIVE or PASSIVE and then is rewritten in the opposite voice.

1. The quarterback completed ten passes. (ACTIVE)
   Ten passes were completed by the quarterback. (PASSIVE)
2. A good time was had by everyone. (PASSIVE)
   Everyone had a good time. (ACTIVE)
3. The band gave a concert last night. (ACTIVE)
   A concert was given by the band last night. (PASSIVE)
4. The building was shaken by the mild earthquake. (PASSIVE)
   The mild earthquake shook the building. (ACTIVE)
5. His great success surprised everyone. (ACTIVE)
   Everyone was surprised by his great success. (PASSIVE)

# Chapter 8: More About Verbs

*Answers to questions on page 180.*

### 5. Progressive Verb Tenses

The following sentences have been rewritten, changing the verb from the present tense to the **present progressive** and then the **past progressive**.

1.  The tree branch **is scraping** against my window.
    The tree branch **was scraping** against my window.
2.  We **are rehearsing** for the spring program.
    We **were rehearsing** for the spring program.
3.  My brother **is competing** in a relay race.
    My brother **was competing** in a relay race.
4.  All the snow **is melting** from the trees.
    All the snow **was melting** from the trees.
5.  The chipmunk **is scurrying** across the lawn.
    The chipmunk **was scurrying** across the lawn.

### 6. Perfect Tenses

The following sentences have been rewritten, changing the verb from the past tense to  the **present perfect** and then the **past perfect**.

1.  I **have carried** all the boxes into the garage.
    I **had carried** all the boxes into the garage.
2.  We **have watched** for the bus to arrive.
    We **had watched** for the bus to arrive.
3.  My family **has gone** from Chicago to Cleveland.
    My family **had gone** from Chicago to Cleveland.
4.  Ellen **has captured** her runaway turtle.
    Ellen **had captured** her runaway turtle.
5.  The movers **have taken** all the furniture out of the house.
    The movers **had taken** all the furniture out of the house.

# Chapter 8: More About Verbs

*Answers to questions on page 181.*

### 7. Using Irregular Verbs

Each sentence is rewritten, changing the verb from the base form to the **past tense**.

1. They **caught** the four o'clock bus yesterday.
2. The small boat **sank** in the storm.
3. My friends **left** before I was able to see them again.
4. He **threw** out a lot of good stuff.
5. Somebody **drank** all the chocolate milk.

### 8. Principal Parts of Irregular Verbs

The principal parts are given for each of the irregular verbs. The verb *choose* was already given as an example.

| Present | Present Participle | Past | Past Participle |
|---------|--------------------|------|-----------------|
| choose | choosing | chose | chosen |
| do | doing | done | done |
| fly | flying | flew | flown |
| think | thinking | thought | thought |
| sing | singing | sang | sung |
| teach | teaching | taught | taught |

# Chapter 8: More About Verbs

*Answers to questions on page 182.*

### 9. Recognizing Participles and Gerunds

All participles and gerunds are underlined, and an arrow is drawn from each participle to the word it modifies. At the end of each sentence, use of the underlined word as a participle or a gerund is indicated.

1. <u>Juggling</u> is his favorite hobby. (gerund)

2. Their <u>speeding</u> car almost ran off the road. (participle)

3. His favorite exercises are <u>jogging</u> and <u>swimming</u>. (gerunds)

4. Our team suffered another <u>humiliating</u> defeat. (participle)

5. The <u>crumbling</u> stone wall was more than 100 years old. (participle)

### 10. Using Participles and Gerunds

Certain words were printed in boldface in the original sentences. Each word is used as a participle (adjective) or as a gerund (noun), depending on each situation. At the end of each sentence, the use of the word is indicated.

1. The **blistering** heat made it impossible to keep walking. (participle)
2. **Installing** the new faucet was not very difficult. (gerund)
3. That is not a very **convincing** argument. (participle)
4. **Wandering** herds of buffalo roamed the plains. (participle)
5. My dog spends most of his time **eating** and **sleeping**. (gerunds)

# *Chapter 9: More About Sentences*

*Answers to questions on page 221.*

**Diagramming Simple Sentences**

Each sentence is diagrammed to show the subject, the verb, and the sentence complement on the base line.

1.  We moved the table into the garage.

    | We | moved | table |
    |----|-------|-------|

2.  Mr. Edwards is the mayor of our town.

    | Mr. Edwards | is \ mayor |
    |-------------|------------|

3.  They cleared all the trash out of the alley.

    | They | cleared | trash |
    |------|---------|-------|

4.  This book is extremely interesting.

    | book | is \ interesting |
    |------|------------------|

# *Chapter 9: More About Sentences*

*Answers to questions on page 222.*

### Diagramming Compound Sentences

Each compound sentence is diagrammed to show the subject, the verb, and the sentence complement on the base line for each part of the sentence.

1. The trip was fun, and we visited many places.

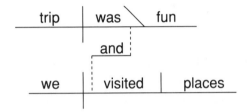

2. The outfielder caught the ball, but the runner scored a run anyway.

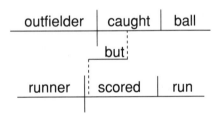

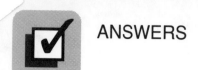 

# *Chapter 9: More About Sentences*

*Answers to questions on page 222.*

3. Mrs. Gomez is my teacher, and she is also our basketball coach.

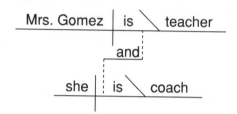

4. The test was difficult, but I got a good grade.

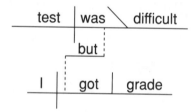

# *Chapter 9: More About Sentences*

*Answers to questions on page 223.*

**Clauses and Complex Sentences**

For each complex sentence, the *independent clause* is written first and the *dependent clause* is written below it.

1. They stopped for pizza after the game ended.
   INDEPENDENT: They stopped for pizza
   DEPENDENT: after the game ended.

2. When we went on vacation, we traveled through four states in one day.
   INDEPENDENT: we traveled through four states in one day.
   DEPENDENT: When we went on vacation,

3. He finished the puzzle before I knew what had happened.
   INDEPENDENT: He finished the puzzle
   DEPENDENT: before I knew what had happened.

4. After the storm ended, the streets were flooded.
   INDEPENDENT: the streets were flooded.
   DEPENDENT: After the storm ended,

# *Chapter 9: More About Sentences*

*Answers to questions on page 223.*

**Appositives**

Each pair of short sentences is rewritten as a single sentence using an **appositive**. The appositive is in italics.

1. Tom's dad let us see inside a plane. Tom's dad is *an airline pilot.*
   Tom's dad, *an airline pilot,* let us see inside a plane.

2. The giraffe eats leaves from the tops of trees. The giraffe is *a long-necked animal.*
   The giraffe, *a long-necked animal,* eats leaves from the tops of trees.

3. My horse has a long mane and tail. My horse is *a palomino named Beauty.*
   My horse, *a palomino named Beauty,* has a long-mane and tail.

4. My friend helped me when I needed it most. My friend is *Karen.*
   My friend *Karen* helped me when I needed it most.

# *Chapter 9: More About Sentences*

*Answers to questions on page 224.*

**Correcting Mistakes in Sentences**

1.  Run-on sentences and sentence fragments are rewritten as two *simple sentences*. Words in boldface have been added to complete the fragments.

    1.  First we flew to Chicago then we drove to Milwaukee.
        First we flew to Chicago. Then we drove to Milwaukee.

    2.  We asked for directions they told us which way to go.
        We asked for directions. They told us which way to go.

    3.  They played baseball for a while. then football.
        They played baseball for a while. Then **they played** football.

    4.  The first show was good I didn't like the other one.
        The first show was good. I didn't like the other one.

    5.  John finished his homework. went to see his friend.
        John finished his homework. **Then he** went to see his friend.

2.  Run-on sentences are changed to **compound sentences** by adding a comma and the word *and* or *but*.

    1.  John watched the movie for a while, **but** he didn't like it.
    2.  They waited for a while, **and** then they left.
    3.  I saw him across the street, **but** he didn't see me.
    4.  Evan watched the game, **and** Roy watched it, too.
    5.  Bill and I went to the zoo, **and** we saw a lot of animals.

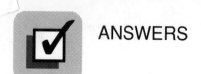 

# Chapter 9: More About Sentences

*Answers to questions on page 225.*

**3.** Sentence fragments and complete sentences are combined to form a **compound sentence**. Words in boldface have been added to complete the fragments whenever necessary.

    1. Bill tried very hard. but didn't win.
       Bill tried very hard, but **he** didn't win.

    2. We asked them to go. they didn't want to.
       We asked them to go, but they didn't want to.

    3. My friends met me after school. went to play ball.
       My friends met me after school, and **we** went to play ball.

    4. We left an hour early. still didn't get there on time.
       We left an hour early, but **we** still didn't get there on time.

    5. There was a boy named Tom. wanted to play football.
       There was a boy named Tom, and **he** wanted to play football.

# *Chapter 10: Word Study*

*Answers to questions on pages 250, 251.*

**1.** The prefix *in-*, *im-*, *il-*, or *ir-* is added to make each boldfaced word a negative. The article has also been changed in one instance.

  1.  Most of his answers were **incorrect**.
  2.  This handwriting is completely **illegible**.
  3.  They are often very **impatient** while they are waiting.
  4.  That was *an* **irresponsible** way to deal with the problem.

**2.** The prefix *com-*, *col-*, or *con-* has been added to each word in boldface.

  1.  They used signal lights to **communicate** with the ship.
  2.  May I **collaborate** with someone on this project?
  3.  I need to **concentrate** on finishing my homework.
  4.  Is the **committee** going to have another meeting?

**3.** This list of words beginning with prefixes was given:

  affect   approve   accept   assume   attend

The correct word is added in boldface in each sentence.

  1.  Please **accept** my apology for the mistake.
  2.  The bad weather will probably **affect** their travel plans.
  3.  Will you be able to **attend** all the meetings?
  4.  I hope they will **approve** my application.
  5.  You shouldn't **assume** that things won't turn out well.

**4.** After each word, the prefix and its meaning are given.
  1.  supervise: *super-* (over, above)
  2.  expel: *ex-* (from, out of)
  3.  implicate: *im-* (in, into)
  4.  extravagant: *extra-* (above, over)
  5.  intermediate: *inter-* (between, among)
  6.  propose: *pro-* (forward, before)
  7.  submerge: *sub-* (under, below)
  8.  immigrant: *im-* (in, into)
  9.  attract: *at-*, from *ad-* (to, at)
  10.  suppose: *sup-*, from *sub-* (under, below)

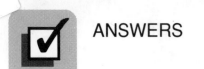

# Chapter 10: Word Study

*Answers to questions on pages 251, 252.*

**5.** Each definition is followed by the word it defines. Each word begins with the prefix *uni-, bi-, tri-, dec-,* or *cent-*.

1. Able to speak two languages: **bilingual**
2. A figure with ten sides: **decagon**
3. Containing three parts: **triple**
4. One hundred years: **century**
5. Something formed by joining several things into one: **union**
6. Consisting of two parts: **binary**

**6.** The suffixes *-er* or *-ment* are used with the words in boldface to derive nouns from verbs.

1. He'll probably be late because he is a heavy **sleeper**.
2. We haven't yet received **payment** for that **shipment**.
3. She is a good **golfer** and an excellent **swimmer**.
4. The **treatment** has enabled him to recover completely.

**7.** The suffixes *-ant* and *-ent* are used with the words in boldface to derive nouns from verbs.

1. He was a **correspondent** for a big newspaper.
2. The **occupant** of the room has already left.
3. The scientist and his **assistant** discovered the vaccine.
4. Will this insect **repellent** keep the bugs away?

**8.** The noun suffix *-ion* is added to each word originally given.

1. rotation
2. collection
3. attention
4. invention
5. protection
6. discussion
7. translation
8. reception

**9.** The adjective suffix *-ive* is added to each of the following words.

1. creative
2. defensive
3. selective
4. receptive
5. decisive
6. persuasive

# INDEX

Page numbers in **boldface** refer to the **Punctuation Guide** on pages 253–262. All other numbers refer to pages within the book.

# INDEX

# INDEX

# INDEX

# INDEX